AF703236

The 24-Hour Historical Drama with ChatGPT

Andrew Parry

Published by Andrew Parry, 2025.

While every precaution has been taken in the preparation of this book, the publisher assumes no responsibility for errors or omissions, or for damages resulting from the use of the information contained herein.

THE 24-HOUR HISTORICAL DRAMA WITH CHATGPT

First edition. April 17, 2025.

Copyright © 2025 Andrew Parry.

ISBN: 979-8227709974

Written by Andrew Parry.

Table of Contents

Unlocking the Power of Historical Drama with ChatGPT

Historical drama is where imagination and research collide in the most fascinating way. It's not just about placing characters in powdered wigs or Victorian corsets, it's about giving life to an era—reviving its politics, its belief systems, its culture, and its humanity through narrative. When done right, historical drama doesn't feel like a dusty old textbook. It feels alive. The emotions are real. The struggles are raw. And ChatGPT can help you get there faster, deeper, and with more creative control than ever before. This chapter is all about how to unlock that power.

Before diving into the writing, you need to understand what makes historical drama so irresistible. It's not just the costumes or the grand architecture, though those are nice. It's the stakes. History was often brutal, uncertain, and full of change. These kinds of conditions create powerful conflict. You're writing about people trapped in times of revolution, war, religious oppression, societal transformation, or cultural upheaval. You don't need to invent the drama—it's already built into the time period. That's why historical drama is such a strong foundation for powerful storytelling.

Now enter ChatGPT. You might be thinking, "But AI doesn't know how to write from the heart." The truth is, it writes from your heart—through your prompts. The emotional depth of your story comes from your vision, but ChatGPT can help shape the bones of the story, fill out research, structure scenes, suggest dialogue, and help maintain the tone of the era. It's not a replacement for your voice. It's a writing partner that never sleeps.

One of the fastest ways to get started with ChatGPT is by prompting it to generate a list of powerful moments in history that are packed with dramatic potential. You don't need to be a history professor. You just need a starting point. Ask it for events that shaped a nation or changed the fate of a group of people. You can narrow it down by geography, decade, cultural group, or theme. Ask it, "Give me ten powerful untold historical events from 19th-century Japan," or "List lesser-known but emotionally rich moments in 16th-century England." ChatGPT will throw out sparks—and one of them might ignite your imagination.

Once you've locked onto a moment in time, the next step is crafting your characters. In historical drama, characters aren't just people—they're representations of the culture, limitations, and hopes of their era. With ChatGPT, you can build character profiles that are era-accurate, asking questions like, "What would a woman of lower-class birth in 18th-century France believe about her place in the world?" You can use these prompts to explore character psychology, social roles, and even inner conflicts born of the era's values.

From there, ChatGPT helps you brainstorm the beats of your plot. What's important here is not to just retell a historical event but to show the human cost or triumph that emerged from it. Ask ChatGPT to help you outline a three-act structure based on emotional turning points rather than just historical ones. For example, rather than just, "The king was deposed," the beats become, "The protagonist sees her family torn apart by the king's decision, joins a rebel cause, and eventually watches that cause lose its soul."

The power of ChatGPT in this genre is how quickly it can shift gears with you. Let's say you've written a scene and you're not sure the tone feels right. You can paste the scene in and say, "Make this feel more desperate, like the character is on the verge of collapse." Or, "Rewrite this in the tone of an epic poem without losing the meaning." ChatGPT lets you experiment with tone, pacing, voice, and rhythm in real-time.

Another powerful way to use ChatGPT is for cultural and atmospheric detail. Historical fiction lives or dies by its authenticity. Readers and viewers can forgive the odd creative liberty, but not a character drinking coffee in

9th-century Europe or using slang that hadn't been invented yet. ChatGPT can instantly give you information on clothing, cuisine, architecture, transportation, language, and even belief systems of the time. If you're stuck trying to describe a setting or wondering what your characters would be eating at a feast, ChatGPT can generate vivid imagery or historically accurate detail in seconds.

But here's the most powerful part of it all—ChatGPT lets you write faster. And that matters in a genre where research and revision can otherwise slow you down. The faster you can sketch a scene, test a character's voice, or map out a subplot, the more you can focus on shaping the emotional journey. You can write an entire first draft of a historical drama in a single day because you're not stopping every five minutes to look something up or rework a scene that doesn't flow. ChatGPT becomes your idea generator, researcher, and rough-draft co-pilot.

Let's say you want to write a story set during the fall of Constantinople in 1453. That's a rich, complex event. You don't need to start with a history book. Ask ChatGPT to summarize the event in five paragraphs, then ask it what kinds of people lived through that siege. What did they believe? What kinds of decisions did they have to make under pressure? Suddenly, you've got a world of conflict, hope, betrayal, and sacrifice to work with. And because ChatGPT is conversational, you can keep digging deeper with each follow-up question.

This doesn't mean you let AI write the story for you. Historical drama still needs your perspective. You're the one who feels which character arcs are most meaningful. You decide whether the story is about the pain of exile, the corruption of leadership, the resilience of faith, or the journey of a forgotten figure finally remembered. ChatGPT simply helps you explore those angles at lightning speed, so you can get to the writing that matters.

Historical drama can be one of the most rewarding genres to write because it teaches the writer just as much as it teaches the audience. You walk in the shoes of people who lived through revolutions, oppression, disasters, and miracles. You find that they aren't so different from us. And ChatGPT lets you bring those stories to life with clarity, confidence, and incredible momentum.

So unlock that potential. Don't let the size of history intimidate you. With your vision and ChatGPT's speed, you can breathe new life into the past and tell stories that speak just as powerfully to the present. That's how you unlock the power of historical drama. And that's how you begin to write yours—today.

Finding the Perfect Historical Moment to Tell Your Story

The foundation of any great historical drama lies in the moment it's set. And by "moment," we're not just talking about a year or a date. We're talking about the emotional pressure point in history that cracks open the door for a compelling story. The truth is, not every historical period is ripe for drama—and not every dramatic event will suit your style, voice, or goals as a storyteller. That's why this chapter is all about finding that perfect moment, and how to use ChatGPT to unearth it in a way that saves you hours and gives you storytelling gold.

You don't need to start with a textbook or a library to find your historical backdrop. You need to start with what you're curious about. Is there a time in history that's always felt magnetic to you? Maybe it's ancient Rome or feudal Japan. Maybe it's the Harlem Renaissance or the Cold War. Start there. Your personal interest is your compass. Passion drives perspective, and historical drama is all about infusing perspective into historical fact. You're not just retelling events—you're shaping them through a lens only you can provide.

Once you've locked in a general area, you want to zoom in. History spans millennia, but your story needs to unfold in a tight frame. That frame is a moment of conflict, change, or transformation. So instead of saying, "I want to write something during the American Revolution," try asking, "What was happening the week before the Declaration of Independence was signed?" or "What was life like for a British soldier realizing the war was lost?" These kinds of questions bring you closer to the drama.

This is where ChatGPT becomes a powerful tool. You can ask it for summaries of specific historical events or moments of upheaval, filtered by location, social class, gender, or theme. Try prompts like, "Tell me about five moments of major cultural upheaval in 19th-century China," or "Give me a list of dramatic but lesser-known events in European history between 1500 and 1600." ChatGPT will deliver quick, focused starting points—some of which you may never have heard of—and every single one could be a portal into a unique narrative.

Let's say you land on the fall of the Berlin Wall. A major event, yes—but you want to write a drama, not a documentary. So you ask ChatGPT, "What kinds of ordinary people were affected most by the fall of the Berlin Wall?" or "What personal stories emerged during the days right before and after it fell?" You'll begin to see the human face of the event, which is what you're really writing about. The politics and dates give it structure. The people give it life.

One method that works surprisingly well is to pick a theme first, then go hunting for a historical moment that mirrors it. Maybe you want to write about betrayal, resilience, forbidden love, identity, or the cost of ambition. You can ask ChatGPT, "What are some historical moments that center around betrayal?" or "Which time periods were defined by identity crises or border shifts?" This turns your personal storytelling interest into a historical framework with built-in emotional tension.

You also want to think visually. Historical drama works best when the setting becomes a character in the story. Think of the misty Scottish Highlands during a rebellion. Think of plague-ridden Florence during the Renaissance. Think of bombed-out London during World War II. Ask ChatGPT for "visually rich historical settings that could serve as metaphors for change" or "ten unique historical backdrops that evoke isolation, pressure, or freedom." The answer may give you not just a time period, but a tone.

Another trick is to blend the personal with the epic. Ask ChatGPT for "overlooked roles in major historical events," like the children of revolutionaries, servants of political leaders, midwives during an outbreak, or artisans during an empire's collapse. These aren't the main figures we learn about in school, but they're the exact kind of characters who make for unforgettable drama. The story of Napoleon has been told many times, but what about the woman who secretly translated enemy plans and watched her country fall anyway?

You can also narrow your historical search by asking ChatGPT for conflicts where the outcome could have gone either way. These are the dramatic tipping points where tension runs high. A single decision, a single act, or a single betrayal could shift the course of history. That kind of suspense is storytelling gold. Whether it's the Cuban Missile Crisis, the Gunpowder Plot, or the last days of the Incan Empire, you're looking for moments when the world held its breath.

Don't underestimate the power of the obscure. The beauty of using ChatGPT is that it can dig up events that aren't in the spotlight but are still filled with potential. Ask for "little-known revolts, natural disasters, love affairs, political scandals, or migrations in the 1700s," and you might find yourself writing about a rebellion that happened in one city but echoed across a continent. Your readers or viewers don't need to know the moment beforehand. They just need to feel that it matters.

Sometimes, the story isn't in the big event but in what comes before or after it. Maybe your drama unfolds during the lead-up to war, when rumors spread and allegiances fracture. Or perhaps it's the aftermath, when survivors are forced to rebuild lives they didn't expect to still be living. Ask ChatGPT for "emotional consequences of the Partition of India" or "what daily life was like after the fall of the Western Roman Empire." These follow-up questions can lead to deeper, more human stories.

If you're writing a screenplay or novel, the pacing of your historical moment matters too. Some events explode in a single day, like assassinations or riots. Others simmer over weeks, like a siege or trial. Choose a pace that suits the story you want to tell. ChatGPT can break down the timeline for you, giving you day-by-day details if needed, so you can plan scenes with emotional crescendo in mind.

By the end of this process, you should have your moment. It might be a single day in the French Revolution. It might be a month in a remote African kingdom under colonial rule. It might be an hour before the Titanic hit the iceberg. What matters is that it sparks something in you—and that it gives your characters room to struggle, change, and grow. ChatGPT won't choose the moment for you. But it will help you uncover possibilities you never knew existed.

That's how you find the perfect historical moment. You follow your passion, let ChatGPT broaden your reach, and then narrow it all back down to a time and place that demands to be written. Once you've found that, you've got your foundation. The rest of the story is waiting to be built on top of it.

Starting with the End: Why the Climax Guides Everything

When you sit down to write a historical drama, it's tempting to begin at the beginning. You might feel drawn to open your story with a character's birth, the start of a revolution, or the moment a world begins to crumble. But the most powerful way to structure your story is actually by doing the opposite. Start with the end. Start with the climax—the emotional explosion, the irreversible decision, the fateful betrayal or bittersweet victory that changes everything. When you begin by imagining the final destination, you create a story that moves with purpose. You know where you're going, so you can guide every character, scene, and line of dialogue to serve that outcome. And in historical drama, where there's already so much happening, this kind of focus can be your creative lifeline.

The climax is the heart of your story. It's not just the biggest moment, it's the emotional payoff. It's when everything your characters have believed, feared, or fought for comes crashing into reality. In historical drama, the climax often sits inside the storm of a real historical moment—an execution, a declaration, a collapse, a march, a betrayal—but it has to be deeply personal too. The audience has to feel it in the chest, not just understand it with the mind. So as a writer, it helps to ask: what does the climax *do* to your characters?

Maybe it breaks them. Maybe it transforms them. Maybe it exposes who they really are. When you define that, you suddenly have a compass that makes everything before it—every scene, every line, every decision—about building up to that emotional impact. That's why we start with the end. Because once you've nailed the ending, the rest of the story becomes a map you reverse-engineer.

Using ChatGPT to structure from the climax backward is a game-changer. You can say, "Help me outline a story where a noblewoman betrays her kingdom to save her child, set during the fall of the Aztec Empire." Within seconds, you can get a list of emotional beats and historical details that help you walk backward from that betrayal to the first scene. You can dig deeper too. Ask ChatGPT, "What would cause a noblewoman to choose family over loyalty in that setting?" Now you're building layers—character motivation, political context, personal stakes—all rooted in that final moment.

Starting with the end also helps with pacing. One of the hardest things in writing historical drama is keeping the story tight when the real world is full of sprawling events and complex social systems. You can get lost in the richness of the setting and forget to move the story forward. But if you know the climax, you can ask yourself at every turn: does this scene bring us closer to that moment? Does this interaction add emotional weight to the ending? If the answer is no, you know to trim or reshape it. ChatGPT can even help with this kind of self-editing. Paste in your scene and ask, "Does this help set up a climax where the protagonist is betrayed by their own son?" Let it offer suggestions. Use them or ignore them. But the tool will always bring you back to the structure.

Here's a technique that works beautifully with ChatGPT: once you know your climax, ask for three possible opening scenes that would thematically mirror or contrast with that ending. For example, if your climax is a priest being excommunicated for protecting a heretic, maybe the story opens with him being praised for his faith in a crowded cathedral. The contrast sets up a powerful arc. Or maybe it opens with him hesitating to burn forbidden books, showing the seed of rebellion that will grow until the final act. ChatGPT can help you test these emotional openings quickly, without committing hours to drafting each one.

Starting with the end also gives your characters stronger arcs. You already know where they'll land—disillusioned, empowered, shattered, awakened—so you can build them from the inside out. Ask ChatGPT, "What would a young soldier have to experience to become the man who orders his best friend's execution in Act Three?" It will give you formative experiences, relationships, traumas, and choices that push the character forward. Suddenly, every step of the story feels inevitable, which is exactly what you want in drama. You want the climax to feel shocking *and* like the only possible outcome.

Another reason starting with the climax is so effective in historical drama is because it creates suspense, even when the audience knows the ending. That's a unique feature of the genre. People might know that the Titanic sinks or that Marie Antoinette is executed, but they don't know *how* your version will get there. They don't know how your characters will suffer, resist, fall in love, betray one another, or cling to hope along the way. So when you write from the climax backward, you're not spoiling the story. You're crafting the emotional journey that makes a known ending feel brand new.

There's also a creative safety net in this approach. If you're ever stuck—if a character feels flat, or a subplot goes nowhere—you can look at the climax and recalibrate. Ask, "How does this choice build toward the moment where everything falls apart?" Or, "Why would this character's actions here lead them to that final decision?" You're never wandering aimlessly. You're always climbing toward the peak, even if the path gets rocky.

One of the best prompts you can use is, "I want to write a historical drama where the climax is [insert idea]. What are the emotional and narrative threads I need to plant in Act One and Two to make it feel earned?" ChatGPT will map out the setups and payoffs that turn your ending into a thunderclap instead of a whisper. And once you've got that structure, you can fill it in with your style, your research, your voice.

If you're writing a novel, screenplay, or even a short story, starting with the end is also a time-saver. It helps you write faster and with more clarity. You're not guessing what happens next—you're sculpting a path toward a moment you already understand. Every paragraph becomes a step toward impact. Every choice builds pressure. ChatGPT accelerates this even more by helping you flesh out backstory, develop character arcs, and explore consequences—all while staying grounded in the goal.

At the end of the day, historical drama isn't about retelling what happened. It's about *why* it mattered. And that meaning usually crystallizes in the climax. That's the moment that haunts the reader, breaks the viewer, or lingers in the mind long after the final line. It's not just an ending. It's the moment when history and humanity collide—and your job is to build everything around it.

So don't start with the beginning. Start with the ending. Let it guide your structure, fuel your characters, shape your research, and power your pace. Use ChatGPT like a story architect, feeding it the final blueprint so it can help you build backward with confidence. When you do this, you don't just write a historical drama. You write one that hits hard, lingers long, and feels like it was always meant to be.

Turning Real Events into Powerful Fiction

One of the most exciting things about writing historical drama is knowing that you don't have to make up the world—it's already there, written in the dusty corners of time, filled with chaos, beauty, cruelty, and transformation. But that doesn't mean you're just repeating what's in a history book. Your job as a storyteller is to take those real events and breathe fiction into them, to explore the emotional truth behind the dates, and to give voice to the people who lived through history but were never heard. That's where the real magic happens. And with ChatGPT by your side, turning real events into compelling fiction becomes a much smoother, faster, and more inspired process.

The key to doing this well is realizing that history is the skeleton, and fiction is the flesh. You don't change the bones—unless you want to—but you dress them with characters, relationships, secrets, fears, and moments of personal triumph or tragedy. You find the heartbeat of the event. If you're writing about the fall of Troy, the bones are war, betrayal, and a burning city. The flesh might be a mother trying to save her children, or a soldier who questions whether the war was ever worth it. You're taking what really happened and asking, "What did this feel like?"

The first thing you want to do is choose your historical event. Not every moment in history needs to be fictionalized. Some are well-documented and need no embellishment. Others are dry, overly bureaucratic, or emotionally flat. So when you pick an event, look for one that already contains drama—conflict, power struggles, shifting alliances, moral dilemmas, or personal stakes. If it's got tension built in, you're already halfway to a story. If you're unsure where to begin, use ChatGPT to ask for "real historical events that are rich in emotion, conflict, and transformation." You'll get a list of ideas that are already bursting with narrative potential.

Once you've got your event, the next step is deciding how close you want to stay to the truth. This is entirely up to you. You might write a story that's meticulously accurate, with real people and real dialogue based on letters or speeches. Or you might change names, compress timelines, invent characters, or imagine what happened behind closed doors. Fiction allows you that freedom. What matters is emotional authenticity. As long as your story feels true to the spirit of the time, you're doing your job.

This is where ChatGPT becomes your best writing partner. You can say, "Help me fictionalize the story of a nurse working during the 1918 Spanish Flu," and it will give you character profiles, potential conflicts, and emotional arcs. Or you can go further and say, "What kinds of moral dilemmas might a nurse face during the Spanish Flu if she was secretly treating people the government abandoned?" Now you're not just telling history—you're exploring the emotional and ethical undercurrents that fiction thrives on.

Another powerful trick is to zoom in. Historical events are often massive in scale—wars, revolutions, migrations—but you don't have to tell the whole story. In fact, you shouldn't. The more intimate your lens, the more powerful your drama becomes. Take one corner of the event. One street. One household. One person. Show how the larger event reshapes their world. Ask ChatGPT to help you brainstorm "a fictional story about a baker in Berlin the night the Wall went up," and you'll get a narrative that focuses on humanity rather than headlines.

Sometimes, the best stories come from the gaps in the record. History doesn't preserve everything. There are blank spaces, unanswered questions, and disputed facts. That's your opening. Where history is silent, fiction can speak. Ask ChatGPT what's not known about a particular event. Say, "What are the historical mysteries or uncertainties surrounding the Boston Tea Party?" or "What do historians still debate about Joan of Arc's trial?" These uncertainties are fertile ground for imagination. You can create a narrative that explores the what-ifs, the unseen, and the emotionally plausible.

Dialogue is another area where you'll rely on fiction to bring reality to life. Historical records rarely give us conversations—at least not the kind that feel intimate, conflicted, or vulnerable. So your job is to create speech that feels real within the time period. You don't want to write in full-blown period slang or archaic phrasing that alienates readers. Instead, find a balance. Ask ChatGPT to help you write dialogue that feels historically grounded but still emotionally accessible. Try a prompt like, "Write a tense conversation between a French revolutionary and his aristocratic sister on the eve of her arrest." The AI can help you test tone, structure, and emotional beats in a matter of minutes.

You also want to consider who tells the story. Historical events often focus on the winners, the powerful, or the ones who left the most records. But fiction allows you to write from the margins. What does the fall of Rome look like through the eyes of a slave? What does the American Civil War feel like to a child too young to understand it? These perspectives are often the most powerful—and they haven't been told a thousand times before. Ask ChatGPT for "unusual or overlooked perspectives on the Black Death" or "a fictional character who could've lived through the Great Fire of London but been left out of the history books." The more unexpected your viewpoint, the fresher your story will feel.

Another technique is to frame your story around a personal question. What does this event mean to your character? What does it challenge in them? What does it awaken or destroy? These questions pull the historical into the emotional realm. ChatGPT can help you explore these inner arcs. Say, "Build a story about a man who loses his faith during the Holocaust but finds meaning in saving others." Now you're telling a deeply personal story set against a historical backdrop—fiction born from fact, shaped by emotion.

You're also allowed to be playful, daring, and even speculative. Some of the best historical fiction takes real events and asks, "What if this had happened instead?" You don't have to stay loyal to the facts if your story demands a twist. Maybe a famous figure survived when they were supposed to die. Maybe an empire collapsed not because of war but because of something supernatural or symbolic. You're writing fiction, after all. Just be intentional about your choices. Ask ChatGPT to help you explore alternative endings or outcomes that feel emotionally satisfying even if they're not historically accurate.

So what's the takeaway? When you turn real events into fiction, you're not bound by rules—you're guided by resonance. You're writing the story behind the headlines, the emotion behind the monument, the humanity behind the war. History gives you the framework. Fiction gives you the voice. And with ChatGPT, you can explore all angles quickly, test out character arcs, build dialogue, and layer in meaning without getting stuck in research quicksand.

The goal is never to replace history. It's to engage with it. To respond to it. To create something that feels true even if the facts have been reshaped. And the better you are at doing that, the more your historical drama will move readers, stay in their memory, and leave them feeling like they've not just learned something—but felt something. That's the power of turning real events into powerful fiction.

Choosing a Time Period That Grips the Reader

Picking the right time period for your historical drama is like picking the right kind of wood to build a fire—it determines whether your story just smoulders or fully catches fire in the reader's imagination. The right era gives your characters weight, your story tension, and your themes an unmistakable echo through time. It's not about choosing a famous century or defaulting to whatever period gets the most screen time. It's about finding the emotional chemistry between the story you want to tell and the world in which it can naturally unfold. And the best part? You don't need to be a historian to get it right. With your curiosity, some creative intention, and the help of ChatGPT, you can find the perfect time period to grip your readers or viewers from page one.

The first place to start is your own gut. What periods of history already fascinate you? Is there a particular age you've always found romantic, terrifying, mysterious, or exhilarating? There's a reason you feel that pull. Maybe you've always been drawn to the Victorian age because of its elegant repression, or you're fascinated by ancient Egypt's mysticism and dynasties. That gut interest is gold—it means you're more likely to explore, to get curious, to stay committed through the many hours it takes to bring that world to life. Readers can sense that passion. They feel it in every detail.

But passion isn't enough on its own. The time period has to be a good fit for your story's emotional core. Ask yourself what your story is really about. Is it about power and control? Then maybe Renaissance Italy, with its political intrigues and warring families, is a better fit than Medieval France. Is it about freedom and reinvention? Then the American frontier might offer a more symbolic setting than wartime Europe. When the themes of your story match the spirit of the time, your narrative resonates on a deeper level. That's where drama finds its real power.

This is where ChatGPT can be a huge help. You don't need to have a history degree to find a time period that fits your theme. You can ask for "time periods in world history where betrayal led to major shifts in power," or "eras known for dramatic class divides and social injustice." You can even ask for "historical settings where identity and secrecy were matters of life and death." Let ChatGPT give you the options, and see which one sparks your imagination. It's about narrowing down the ocean of history into a handful of powerful story-friendly possibilities.

Another way to approach this is through tone. Think about how you want your story to *feel*. Is it eerie and claustrophobic? Maybe a small medieval town during a witch trial gives you that atmospheric tension. Is it fast-paced and dangerous? Maybe a city on the brink of revolution—Paris in 1789 or Petrograd in 1917—is the backdrop you need. ChatGPT can help you pair emotional tone with historical backdrop. Try prompts like, "List dramatic historical settings that feel intense and urgent," or "What historical time periods would suit a slow-burning psychological drama?" Let the vibe of the period shape the mood of your scenes.

It's also important to consider the level of familiarity your audience might have with the period. Writing about World War II or Ancient Rome means readers are likely walking in with some expectations. That's not necessarily a bad thing—it means your story might instantly feel grounded. But it also means you need to offer something new. Either a unique perspective, an unexpected plot twist, or a character who doesn't fit the usual mold. On the flip side, choosing a lesser-known era gives you more freedom to surprise your audience. They won't see the ending coming because they don't already know the historical arc. ChatGPT can help you strike this balance. Ask for "overlooked but dramatically rich time periods in global history" or "events that had major emotional consequences but are rarely covered in fiction."

When thinking about setting, also ask: what kind of world do I want my characters to be up against? In some eras, the world is the antagonist. It's brutal, chaotic, oppressive. In others, it's shifting, uncertain, full of potential. The environment shapes your characters as much as any villain. Writing about someone coming of age during the Cultural Revolution in China is a very different emotional landscape than someone finding love during the Summer of Love in 1967 San Francisco. ChatGPT can help you dig into the social and emotional climate of different time periods. Ask, "What were the emotional pressures faced by women in early 20th-century Istanbul?" or "What did young artists face during Franco's Spain?" These snapshots can help you understand not just the facts, but the human tension in the era.

And don't forget to think about pacing. Some historical settings lend themselves to slow-burning dramas with internal stakes—stories of moral conflict, quiet rebellion, or secret love. Others have built-in urgency: wars, sieges, pandemics, coups. The time period can act as your built-in engine. A story set during the Blitz has a very different pacing than one set in an isolated monastery in the 12th century. ChatGPT can help with this too. Ask for "historical periods with high-stakes, fast-moving external conflicts" or "settings suitable for introspective, character-driven drama." Tailor the tempo to your narrative.

Language and culture also play a role. Some time periods are easier to write for because the language and worldview are still somewhat accessible to a modern audience. Others require more careful adaptation. If you're writing a 9th-century Norse tale or a story set in the Song Dynasty, you'll need to be conscious of how you translate ideas of family, fate, honor, or love into something today's readers can relate to. ChatGPT is your best research partner here. You can ask, "How did people in Edo-period Japan view honor and duty?" or "What was the role of women in Viking society?" These insights will help you write characters that feel like they belong to their world—while still connecting to ours.

At some point, you'll come across an era that just clicks. It's not just historically rich—it feels emotionally aligned with your vision. When you find it, don't second-guess yourself. Lean into it. Ask ChatGPT to help you build out the world: "Describe the clothing, architecture, and street life of a small Portuguese town in the 1500s," or "What kind of social tensions existed in early 20th-century Mexico City?" Let it help you layer in those period details that will make your story feel lived-in, textured, and real.

Ultimately, choosing a gripping time period means choosing a world with built-in pressure. A world where the stakes are high, the rules are strict or shifting, and your characters have something real to lose. That's where drama lives. That's where your story breathes. And with the right tools—your vision, your instincts, and the speed and depth of ChatGPT—you'll find the perfect era to set it all in motion.

When you get this part right, everything else falls into place. The dialogue has more depth. The setting feels immersive. The conflicts hit harder. So don't rush this decision. Explore the past until something grabs you and doesn't let go. That's when you know you've found your time. And when you do, history stops being old. It becomes urgent. It becomes human. It becomes yours.

Building a Hero Rooted in the Past

Creating a protagonist in a historical drama isn't about designing a hero and then dropping them into a time period like a tourist—it's about weaving them so tightly into their era that they feel like they *belong* to it. Your hero must breathe the air of the past, think in its language, move through its hierarchies, and face its moral dilemmas. When a hero is rooted in the past, every action they take gains meaning, every choice they make carries weight, and every inner conflict becomes a reflection of the world around them. You're not just building a character—you're building a mirror of a moment in history. And with ChatGPT, this becomes a process of discovery that unfolds with clarity and speed.

Start by asking yourself what kind of story you want to tell through this character. What's the emotional core? Is it a story about sacrifice? Rebellion? Redemption? Forbidden love? Survival? The theme you choose should shape not only the character's arc but the context of their birth, their education, their values, and their blind spots. A character rooted in the past has to be a product of their time—but also capable of challenging it. That tension is where historical heroes really shine.

ChatGPT can be your springboard into this kind of character work. You can begin by telling it, "I want to create a female protagonist living in 15th-century Florence who challenges the restrictions placed on women," and it will immediately generate a framework of personality traits, societal limitations, and possible relationships that define her world. You can then shape her according to your own vision—making her softer or harder, more idealistic or more pragmatic—but now you have a cultural anchor. She isn't just a modern woman in a period costume. She's a woman born of that place, struggling against what it means to live inside that history.

Backstory is critical here. Not just where your character comes from, but how they were shaped by the time period. What were the expectations placed on them? What were the opportunities available—or denied? What did they believe about themselves before the story even began? A hero rooted in the past doesn't need to be defined by the dominant ideas of the time, but they do need to *react* to them. If they question authority, it should be because they've experienced its consequences. If they defy a religious or political system, it should come from something personal. ChatGPT can help by offering sample backstories that are era-accurate and emotionally textured. Ask, "What kind of childhood would a lower-class soldier's son have in Tsarist Russia?" or "Describe the worldview of a freed slave living in 1870s America." You're building an inner world that is as detailed as the historical one.

Character flaws become even more powerful in historical drama. Maybe your hero has internalized the biases of their time. Maybe they're loyal to a dying empire. Maybe they're blind to their own privilege. The past gives you room to explore how someone grows *through* outdated ideas, not just in spite of them. You can use ChatGPT to help define these flaws in context. Try, "Give me examples of era-specific flaws for a nobleman in 18th-century France," or "What prejudices would a British colonist in India have in the 19th century?" These flaws aren't there to shame the character—they're there to give them space to evolve, which is what every good drama needs.

Rooting a hero in the past also means designing their motivations based on what was truly at stake in their world. A modern character might want freedom, but what did freedom mean in 1348? Maybe it meant being able to leave your guild. Maybe it meant escaping an arranged marriage. Maybe it meant the power to own land or choose your own apprenticeship. The specifics matter. ChatGPT can help by unpacking what ambition, love, power, or fear looked like in your chosen era. You can ask, "What did upward mobility look like in the Ottoman Empire?" or "What kind of autonomy did women have in 17th-century Persia?" Use this information to shape a protagonist whose desires are historically grounded yet emotionally universal.

Relationships are another important anchor. Who are your hero's parents? Siblings? Mentors? Enemies? In historical drama, relationships are rarely equal, and that inequality creates instant conflict. A servant and their employer. A noblewoman and her handmaid. A general and a conscripted farmer. Power dynamics were everywhere, and your hero's journey will be shaped by how they respond to those dynamics—whether they reinforce them, resist them, or exploit them. ChatGPT can help brainstorm relationship arcs within historical power structures. Ask for, "A tense mentor-student relationship in ancient Athens," or "Ideas for a forbidden romance in a rigid caste society."

Dialogue is where your hero really proves their connection to the past. They don't have to speak in period-perfect prose, but they *shouldn't* sound like they stepped out of a Netflix original either. The language they use should reflect their level of education, their exposure to different cultures, and their station in life. ChatGPT can help you test dialogue for tone and accuracy. Say, "Write a conversation between a 12th-century monk and a merchant about the Crusades," and you'll see how values, speech, and worldview play out in real time. Use that as a guide for writing dialogue that feels lived-in and true to the moment.

Of course, your hero doesn't have to be historically famous. In fact, they probably shouldn't be. Some of the most memorable historical dramas are about fictional characters who live through real events. Their personal journey is what gives meaning to the broader history. You don't need to write about Queen Elizabeth or Genghis Khan. You can write about the people caught in the ripples of their rule—the maid, the farmer, the scribe, the orphan, the outsider. These characters give the audience a way in. They offer a perspective that feels emotionally grounded.

Your protagonist also doesn't have to be "heroic" in the traditional sense. They don't have to lead a rebellion or change the course of history. Sometimes, the quietest acts are the most powerful. A woman refusing to testify against her lover. A boy hiding books during a fascist regime. A man walking away from a family legacy that made him rich but corrupt. ChatGPT can help generate these smaller acts of resistance or transformation, framed within the values of the era. You can say, "Give me subtle but powerful acts of rebellion a Jewish girl might undertake in Nazi-occupied France," or "What kinds of quiet courage might a widow show in feudal Korea?" Let it open doors you hadn't considered.

In the end, building a hero rooted in the past is about balance. You want them to be believable in their world, but not completely trapped by it. You want them to reflect their time, but still surprise the audience. You want them to carry the weight of history, but still chase something personal. When you find that sweet spot—and when you use ChatGPT to test and refine their layers—you get a character who doesn't just exist in a time period. They *embody* it. They challenge it. And through them, your audience gets to live and feel the past in a way no history book could ever offer.

Creating an Antagonist That Defines the Era

In historical drama, the antagonist does far more than block the hero's progress—they often *embody* the world the hero is struggling to survive or change. A great historical antagonist isn't just a villain with a sneer and a sword. They are the face of the system, the ideology, or the belief that needs to be questioned, resisted, or overthrown. Whether it's a cruel monarch, a religious zealot, a war-hardened general, or a wealthy aristocrat dripping with entitlement, the antagonist must speak for the time and challenge the protagonist in a way that brings out the deeper truth of the era. Getting this right transforms your story from a period piece into a living, breathing drama with teeth.

Start with the era itself. Every time period has dominant systems—religion, class, gender roles, imperialism, industry, nationalism—and these systems often favor the powerful. Your antagonist should be plugged into that power in a way that feels both personal and systemic. They don't have to be in a throne room or wearing a crown. They could be a landlord, a military officer, a gatekeeper of tradition, or even a family member. What matters is that they serve as the physical and emotional embodiment of what the protagonist is pushing against.

One way to begin is by identifying the values of the time period. Was it an age of blind faith, rigid honor, patriarchal control, colonial expansion, or class warfare? ChatGPT can help you with this immediately. Ask, "What were the dominant values in 17th-century Spain?" or "Describe the social hierarchy in 18th-century India," and you'll get a snapshot of what your antagonist could represent. From there, shape a character who enforces or profits from that system—and who sees the protagonist's values as a direct threat.

You don't want a one-note villain, though. The strongest historical antagonists aren't evil for the sake of it—they believe in their cause. They are often trying to preserve the world as it is, or return to a version of the world that used to work for them. Ask ChatGPT to help you understand the internal logic of your antagonist. Try, "What motivations would a plantation owner in 1860s Louisiana have for resisting abolition?" or "How would a female inquisitor justify her persecution of accused witches?" You're not creating sympathy necessarily—you're creating complexity. That's what makes your antagonist *real*.

The relationship between your hero and antagonist is central to making this work. In many historical dramas, they start out on the same side or inside the same system. It's only over time that their values diverge. That divergence becomes the drama. Maybe they're siblings from a noble family, with one embracing reform and the other clinging to tradition. Maybe they're teacher and student, mentor and heir, priest and disciple. Use ChatGPT to brainstorm these pairings. Ask, "What's a historically accurate dynamic between a general and his adopted son in Ancient Rome?" or "What tensions might exist between a female scholar and a male religious authority in 15th-century Persia?" The emotional complexity of their connection will elevate the conflict beyond good versus evil.

Sometimes, the antagonist isn't a person at all—but it still helps to personify the conflict. If your story is about a small community resisting industrialization, then the antagonist might be the factory owner. If it's about a girl fighting for education under an oppressive regime, then her school principal becomes the face of that ideology. ChatGPT can help you brainstorm these characters quickly. Ask for "a human representative of religious oppression in 16th-century England" or "a fictional character who could represent economic colonialism in West Africa." Let the AI help you explore different angles until you find one that sparks something in you.

Another way to ground your antagonist in the era is to define what they fear. Fear is one of the most revealing tools in fiction. A man who fears losing his title might uphold a brutal social system. A woman who fears scandal might protect the very patriarchy that oppresses her. An empire that fears rebellion will act violently to suppress even peaceful change. Fear gives your antagonist believable motivation and tragic depth. Use ChatGPT to dig into this. Try prompts like, "What would a feudal lord in 14th-century Japan fear losing the most?" or "Describe the social consequences feared by a noblewoman in 18th-century Russia if her secret was revealed." Those fears will shape your antagonist's actions.

Don't forget that sometimes the antagonist thinks *they* are the hero. This is especially true in historical drama, where morality is a moving target. What we view as oppression today may have been seen as virtue in another era. If you write your antagonist from their own point of view, you'll get a character who isn't just an obstacle, but a dramatic force with their own arc. Ask ChatGPT, "Describe a colonial governor who sees himself as a civilizing force" or "Write a monologue from a medieval inquisitor who believes he's saving souls." The antagonist's version of the truth will make them more unsettling—and more compelling.

In historical drama, the antagonist often has power the protagonist doesn't. That imbalance is part of the tension. But that power can take many forms—social power, financial control, access to weapons, religious authority, or even simply the ability to make decisions without consequence. Define the power imbalance clearly. How does the antagonist use their position to suppress or manipulate the protagonist? And more importantly, how does the protagonist learn to outgrow or outmaneuver that power? That's the engine of your story.

ChatGPT can help you brainstorm specific moments where the antagonist exercises their authority. Try, "Give me examples of how a medieval king might test the loyalty of his knights," or "Describe a courtroom scene where a female activist is interrogated by a high-ranking official during the early 20th-century suffragette movement." Use those moments to build dramatic beats that raise the stakes and push your characters toward transformation.

The final thing to remember is that your antagonist doesn't just reflect the past—they frame it. Through their actions and worldview, the audience understands the cost of living in that era. The cruelty, the pressure, the impossible choices. When your antagonist is fully realized, they become the scaffolding that supports the emotional truth of the story. They force the hero to evolve, and they become the voice of the very thing your protagonist must overcome.

So take your time creating this character. Make them intelligent. Make them dangerous. Make them a product of their time—but not a cliché of it. Let ChatGPT help you test different combinations of background, belief, fear, and influence. You're not just writing a villain. You're writing history's reflection—and through that reflection, your story gains weight, complexity, and power.

Developing Side Characters with Historical Purpose

Side characters in historical drama aren't just there to support the protagonist or move the plot forward—they're your secret weapon for making the past feel alive. When done well, they carry the texture of the era, the color of its contradictions, and the nuances of the society your main character is caught inside. They're not filler. They're a chorus of perspectives. They show the audience what life looks like outside the central conflict, and they add emotional layers and political tension without having to dominate the spotlight. In many ways, they are the world, and building them with intention gives your story dimension that research alone can't provide.

Historical purpose means these side characters are not randomly thrown into the narrative. They have roles that reflect the time they live in. Whether they're servants, scholars, merchants, healers, soldiers, nuns, thieves, or peasants, their function in the story should also mirror their function in society. And their worldviews should come from the values of the era—not from modern sensibilities. That doesn't mean you can't give them depth or agency. It means their goals, fears, and limitations must emerge from the conditions of their environment. When you get that balance right, they not only feel authentic—they elevate your entire story.

One way to start building these characters is to use the protagonist as your lens. Who surrounds them in their everyday life? Who challenges them? Who reinforces the system they're trapped in? Who quietly pushes back? Side characters are a great way to show contrast and reflection. If your hero is a young woman resisting an arranged marriage, you might include an older sister who accepted hers, a maid who envies her choices, and a grandmother who regrets her silence. Each of these characters becomes a thematic echo of the central conflict, revealing how others have coped—or failed to cope—with the same pressures.

With ChatGPT, you can build these characters in seconds and then refine them into deeper personalities. Ask for something simple to start, like, "Give me five historically accurate side characters who might surround a nobleman in 16th-century Venice," or "Suggest a group of villagers living in rural Japan during the Edo period with diverse worldviews." You'll get a list of roles, and then you can dive deeper into each one: What do they believe? What do they want? What do they fear? How do they survive in a world shaped by hierarchy, religion, war, or poverty?

What makes side characters powerful is their relationship to the protagonist's journey. Some will act as catalysts, pushing the hero toward change. Others will be cautionary tales, showing what happens when you don't change. Some will be gatekeepers, blocking the path forward. And a few will be mirrors, holding up uncomfortable truths. You don't need dozens of fully developed characters, but the few you focus on should have a clear purpose in the emotional architecture of your story.

ChatGPT can help by generating character arcs for these roles. Try, "Write a side character arc for a servant who becomes disillusioned with her noble employers during the French Revolution," or "Describe a soldier who begins loyal but becomes sympathetic to the enemy in the Crimean War." You'll quickly see how even a minor character can add weight to the story when their personal evolution reflects or collides with the larger historical backdrop.

Historical side characters also allow you to represent different layers of society. Not everyone in your story needs to be a noble or a general. Sometimes the most fascinating characters are the ones history forgets. The street vendor, the stable boy, the midwife, the prison guard—these characters lived under the weight of history but left little trace. You get to give them a voice. Ask ChatGPT for "historically overlooked professions in 14th-century Cairo" or "unusual jobs in 19th-century London," and you'll get a list of roles that can become springboards for unforgettable personalities.

Diversity within your cast matters too, especially when writing about empires, colonial periods, or port cities where cultures intersected. You can use side characters to explore how people of different faiths, ethnicities, or social standings experienced the same event in radically different ways. A revolution seen by a landowning merchant will not be the same as how it's felt by an indentured servant or an outsider from another country. ChatGPT can help you uncover the global and multicultural dimensions of a time period. Ask, "What immigrant communities lived in 18th-century Paris?" or "What groups were marginalized in the Ottoman Empire during the 1600s?" Use this to add historical truth through your characters.

Don't overlook how powerful silence can be in a side character, either. Sometimes a character doesn't speak much, but their presence alone carries meaning. A loyal bodyguard. A quietly suffering spouse. A prisoner who watches everything but says nothing. The way they interact with the protagonist—through a look, a gesture, a refusal—can become a moment of emotional truth. ChatGPT can help you script these subtle interactions. Try, "Write a silent exchange between a dying soldier and a battlefield nurse in World War I that reveals mutual understanding." The more intentional you are with the smallest characters, the richer your world becomes.

Side characters are also your chance to inject texture and rhythm into the narrative. They provide humor, conflict, perspective, and even exposition when handled well. A bitter tavern keeper can deliver backstory. A cynical friend can cut through the hero's optimism. A religious zealot can deliver the chilling logic of the time period. When each character comes with a piece of the world attached to them, you're no longer just writing about history—you're immersing your audience in it.

Their clothing, mannerisms, and speech should reflect their station. A farmhand shouldn't speak like a royal advisor. A nun might speak in riddles, metaphors, or lines from scripture. A soldier might grunt, curse, or cut straight to the point. Use ChatGPT to test dialogue for each one. Say, "Write a conversation between a Roman slave and a senator," or "Give me an argument between a 19th-century Irish domestic worker and her employer." These little interactions are where characters leap off the page.

At the end of the day, side characters serve two jobs. They build the world, and they deepen the story. When they have purpose, when they are shaped by the historical pressures around them, they do more than decorate the background—they embody the tension and transformation of the time. Whether they live or die, succeed or fall, comfort or betray, they carry your audience deeper into a place where history doesn't feel distant—it feels personal.

So give them time. Let them surprise you. Ask ChatGPT to help you discover their fears, their secrets, their dreams. And then watch as your historical drama takes on new depth, not because of the lead, but because of the lives that circle quietly around them—each one carrying a fragment of the past, and a truth that refuses to be forgotten.

Breathing Life into Forgotten Times

One of the most rewarding things you can do in historical drama is give voice to the eras that time has tried to erase. These are the stories not found in mainstream textbooks or romanticized Hollywood narratives. They're the quiet centuries, the uncelebrated revolutions, the slow-burning changes that happened far from thrones and battlefields. And within them lies gold—because the less explored the time, the more freedom you have to shape something uniquely powerful. But breathing life into forgotten times isn't just about finding obscure settings. It's about learning how to animate them with texture, emotion, and humanity. It's about taking a dusty corner of history and making it burn with life, urgency, and truth.

So how do you start? You begin with curiosity, not with certainty. Forget what you think is historically important. Instead, ask what's emotionally relevant. Forgotten times are usually overlooked because they didn't feature the kind of drama that gets commemorated—giant wars, famous kings, global empires. But maybe what you want to write about isn't the center of power. Maybe it's a rural community cut off from the rest of the world, or an artist's circle that died with its last disciple, or a coastal town on the edge of a failing trade route. These are places where real people lived out full lives—lives worth rediscovering.

ChatGPT is an incredible tool for unlocking these forgotten settings. You can ask it for "lesser-known historical periods with rich storytelling potential" or "obscure yet transformative moments in global history." You'll find moments you've never heard of—maybe a rebellion that lasted three weeks in the Caribbean, or a wave of religious reform in a medieval African kingdom, or a lost civilization buried beneath modern cities. You don't need to know everything about them. You just need a spark of interest—and then, scene by scene, you build the world.

The biggest challenge with obscure time periods is making them feel real to the reader. You're starting from a place of limited shared knowledge. So your job is to immerse the reader through sensory experience. What did the world look like? What were the textures of daily life? What sounds filled the air at dawn or dusk? What did people eat, wear, pray for, fear? These aren't just background details—they're the architecture of your story's emotional landscape. ChatGPT can help you generate sensory-rich descriptions by prompting it with, "Describe a fishing village in 11th-century Scandinavia at dawn," or "What would a feast look like in a small Buddhist monastery in 10th-century China?" From there, you build authenticity one detail at a time.

Another powerful tool in forgotten times is symbolism. Since the reader may not know the events, places, or names, you can guide them through the emotional truth of the world by anchoring key objects or rituals in symbolism. A broken pendant. A forbidden lullaby. A ritual only performed in secret. These elements become emotional shortcuts. They tell the audience, "This matters," even if they've never heard of the setting before. You can ask ChatGPT, "What cultural symbols were used in pre-colonial West Africa to convey strength or shame?" or "Suggest symbolic objects in a story set in the Mongol Empire." Use what resonates.

Don't be afraid to invent, either. Historical fiction allows you to take artistic liberties, especially when dealing with times that left behind few records. As long as your world feels emotionally honest and internally consistent, readers will follow you. It's not about absolute accuracy—it's about believability. When writing about a forgotten time, you're not just recreating what was. You're also imagining what *might have been*. Use ChatGPT to fill in historical gaps with plausible culture, conflict, and character. Try asking, "Invent daily customs for a fictional village under Norse control in Greenland," or "Create three religious beliefs held by an isolated island community in the Indian Ocean during the 13th century."

Side characters become especially important in these stories. Because there may not be familiar reference points, your characters become the audience's only guide to the world. Their relationships, rituals, fears, and habits communicate more than exposition ever could. A father who's ashamed to break a seasonal oath tells you volumes about that culture's spiritual backbone. A widow who weaves a different pattern into every blanket she sells hints at stories hidden in domestic work. Ask ChatGPT to help you create side characters who act as living representations of their time. Try prompts like, "What kinds of community leaders might exist in an indigenous mountain tribe with no written language?" or "Create a group of children with different social roles in a tiny desert outpost in the 12th century."

The forgotten times are also where you'll often find forgotten voices. History tends to spotlight the loudest people in the loudest places—kings, generals, priests. But what about the voices of women, children, slaves, artisans, laborers, prisoners, refugees, or nomads? These voices are often absent not because they were silent, but because no one recorded them. Fiction gives you the power to change that. You get to fill that silence with truth. Ask ChatGPT to suggest "fictional perspectives of marginalized people living through the collapse of a dynasty" or "a story told from the point of view of a deaf child during the Black Death." These characters don't just fill space—they deepen the world by showing us the corners of the past where humanity endured, unseen.

Your antagonist in a forgotten time may also look different. They may not be a singular figure but a force—ignorance, disease, famine, superstition, or even change itself. In remote places, the idea of a villain can take on mythic proportions. A neighbor who betrays the harvest agreement. A clan leader who refuses to embrace new technology. A merchant who introduces foreign coin to a barter economy. ChatGPT can help you invent systemic or symbolic antagonists. Ask for, "Create a belief system that opposes outside contact," or "What fears would an isolated society have toward newcomers bearing gifts and stories?" These challenges form the backdrop for emotionally charged stories of resistance or transformation.

One of the most satisfying outcomes of writing in a forgotten time is that you get to teach through story, without lecturing. You transport your audience somewhere they've never been, show them what it felt like to live and love and suffer there, and in doing so, you make that place real. You connect the present to the past not with facts—but with empathy.

So when you sit down to write, remember that bringing a forgotten time to life doesn't mean digging up every detail—it means finding the pulse of that world and letting it beat through your characters, your imagery, your conflict, and your voice. Let ChatGPT be your lantern. Use it to shine light into those hidden corners of history, to build bridges where records have crumbled, and to turn quiet stories into thunderous drama.

Because once you breathe life into a forgotten time, it's no longer forgotten. It becomes unforgettable.

Getting the Period Details Right with ChatGPT

One of the most intimidating things about writing historical drama is the detail. The clothes. The food. The social customs. The tools, the titles, the transport, the etiquette. It can feel like if you get one little thing wrong, someone somewhere will notice and discredit your whole story. And that fear can freeze your creativity. But here's the truth: you don't need to be an expert in every detail to write convincing historical fiction—you just need to know how to ask the right questions and where to look for answers. That's where ChatGPT becomes a game-changer.

Using ChatGPT to get your period details right is like having a research assistant with an encyclopaedic memory and a limitless work ethic. You can ask for information in seconds that would've taken hours to dig up in books or cross-reference online. And it's not just about facts. ChatGPT can help you shape atmosphere, find cultural nuance, or develop believable objects and actions that fit seamlessly into the world you're building.

The first thing to understand is how to frame your questions. Don't just ask for "life in 18th-century France." That's way too broad. Ask, "What kind of dress would a lower-class Parisian woman wear in winter around 1780?" or "What kind of food might a street vendor sell in a French market during that time?" Be specific. Ask about daily habits, clothing materials, transportation methods, the type of paper people wrote on, what time the sun rose in that region, how children were punished in school. These are the questions that bring a setting to life—not just who ruled at the time.

Let's say you're writing a scene where your character is preparing for a journey. Ask ChatGPT, "How would someone travel from Vienna to Prague in 1600? What kind of carriage would they use? How long would it take? What would they bring with them?" The AI will deliver an answer with context, terminology, and additional suggestions you may not have thought of. It might mention how poor road conditions could delay the trip, or how inns functioned at the time, or how traveling alone could be risky, especially for women. That kind of layered insight can take your scene from generic to immersive.

If you're unsure what kinds of questions to even ask, let ChatGPT guide you. Try, "What kinds of historically accurate sensory details should I include when writing about a port town in 17th-century Spain?" It might return suggestions about the smells of the harbor, the sounds of gulls and sailors shouting in various dialects, the chaos of cargo loading, the layered clothing against the cold sea breeze, or the salt-crusted barrels of preserved fish stacked along the dock. Every one of those details creates mood and credibility.

ChatGPT can also help you build out believable items, rituals, and behaviors. Want to write a dinner scene? Ask, "What would an aristocratic dinner in Russia look like in 1800? What courses would be served? What kind of etiquette would be expected?" You'll not only get a list of food but possibly also insights into silverware usage, expected seating arrangements, and social taboos—like whether servants are allowed to speak or how to address the host.

Another great use of ChatGPT is to fact-check yourself quickly. Let's say you wrote a scene where a character checks the time on a pocket watch in the early 1500s. You might ask, "Would a merchant in Italy in 1520 realistically carry a pocket watch?" and ChatGPT will tell you if it's plausible—or not. That instant verification allows you to move forward with confidence without getting stuck in endless rabbit holes.

But getting the period details right isn't just about technical accuracy. It's also about worldview. What did people believe at the time? What did they fear, admire, ridicule, or aspire to? ChatGPT can help you explore this inner landscape by prompting questions like, "What did people in Medieval England think about illness and the body?" or "What superstitions were common among sailors in the 1700s?" These cultural attitudes will shape your characters' choices in authentic ways and can fuel both conflict and theme.

Let's say you're writing about a young apprentice in Renaissance Florence who becomes disillusioned with the church. Ask ChatGPT, "What religious practices or ideas would this character likely encounter at work or in public life?" or "How would doubts about faith have been viewed socially at that time?" You'll gain insight into not only the practices but the psychological tension surrounding them, which gives your story emotional texture rooted in historical reality.

Another clever use is asking ChatGPT to compare then and now. If you're struggling to frame something in historical terms, ask, "How is education in 17th-century Scotland different from today?" or "What was the role of women in Edo-period Japan compared to modern-day expectations?" This side-by-side lens can help you make your narrative more readable for modern audiences without compromising authenticity.

When it comes to language, you can also ask for era-appropriate phrases or turns of speech. Say you want your characters to sound period-accurate without being unreadable. Ask ChatGPT, "What kind of insults would a nobleman use in 15th-century France?" or "Give me polite greetings and farewells common in the British Regency era." Use these to lace flavor into your dialogue without overwhelming it. Your goal is always clarity first, color second.

And if you want your entire story to breathe authenticity, try having ChatGPT audit your draft. Feed it a scene and ask, "Is anything in this scene anachronistic for 1340s rural England?" or "What elements of this dialogue feel too modern for the 1800s?" This won't replace a historian's eye, but it will catch most obvious slips, give you alternatives, and keep you moving forward without obsessing over every detail.

If you're blending real and fictional elements, you can also use ChatGPT to help shape those fictional additions so they feel seamless within the setting. Suppose you've invented a secret society operating in 17th-century Prague. Ask, "What kind of rituals, symbols, and language might a secret group of scientists use during this time without attracting suspicion?" Now your fantasy detail feels believable because it's built on a foundation of historical logic.

So yes, getting the period details right matters—but it doesn't have to be a burden. With ChatGPT, you're never writing blind. You can dip into the past anytime, ask whatever you need, and instantly enrich your story with detail, texture, and emotional credibility. Don't aim for perfection. Aim for immersion. Give your reader just enough truth to let them surrender to the world you've built. The moment your setting feels lived in, they won't question it—they'll believe it.

Because when the details click, the world comes alive. And when the world feels real, your historical drama becomes more than just a story—it becomes an experience.

Creating Tension between Past and Present

One of the most powerful tools in historical drama is the invisible tug-of-war between the world as it was and the world as we now know it. Even if your story is set entirely in the past, your reader or viewer is experiencing it through the lens of today. That creates tension—quiet, constant, often unspoken—and if you know how to harness it, your narrative will hum with depth and resonance. You're not just telling a story about then. You're forcing the audience to think about *now* in ways they didn't expect.

This tension is at its most effective when it's baked into character conflict, worldview, and theme. You don't need a time-travel device or a narrator from the future to explore it. The very act of watching characters struggle with outdated systems, resist injustice, or cling to belief systems that have since collapsed creates friction. Audiences know what comes next. They know the revolution fails or succeeds. They know the science was wrong or the culture changes. That hindsight creates irony, dread, hope, and sometimes sorrow. The past becomes a mirror held up to the present—and it's cracked in just the right way.

Start by understanding the moral compass of the time you're writing about. What did society reward? What was taboo? What were people forbidden to want, to say, to be? Use ChatGPT to explore this in detail. Ask, "What were the social expectations for a widowed woman in 17th-century Ireland?" or "What kinds of punishments were given to people who questioned the church in 1500s Italy?" Once you know what the rules were, you can create characters who follow them—and others who quietly or violently push against them.

The protagonist is often the voice of conflict between past and present, especially when they resist the worldview they've inherited. But you can deepen the drama by giving that resistance internal stakes. Maybe they *want* to believe what they've been taught, but their experience makes belief impossible. Maybe they feel shame for even questioning the norm. Maybe they're caught between the safety of conformity and the danger of truth. That's where your audience starts leaning in. That's where the tension lives.

Let's say you're writing about a young man in a theocratic society who discovers an ancient manuscript that contradicts his religion. Today's reader might cheer for his rebellion—but in the context of his world, he's a heretic, a threat, a traitor. That dissonance creates drama. Ask ChatGPT to help you imagine the cultural pressure he would face. Try prompts like, "What consequences would a person face for denying divine law in a 10th-century Middle Eastern city?" or "How might a character hide intellectual rebellion in a closed academic system in 17th-century Europe?" The answers won't just build your plot. They'll build the invisible wall your character must climb over, brick by brick.

Another method for exploring this tension is through generational conflict. One of the cleanest ways to express the struggle between old and new is in a conversation between characters of different ages. The older character represents tradition, memory, and legacy. The younger one embodies change, impatience, and risk. You don't need to make one right and the other wrong. Just let the friction speak. Use ChatGPT to write sample conversations or debates. Ask, "Create a dialogue between a mother and daughter in 19th-century Japan about arranged marriage," or "Write an argument between a veteran of the Napoleonic Wars and his pacifist grandson in 1830s France." These emotional exchanges carry the heartbeat of your story's tension.

Symbolism helps, too. Objects that once meant honor, safety, or identity can become sources of shame, fear, or doubt. A family sword that once defended the homeland may now hang like a threat. A sacred text that offered clarity might now feel like a prison. A hairstyle, a tattoo, a piece of clothing—each can reflect the weight of tradition clashing with a character's evolving self. Ask ChatGPT to suggest objects that carried cultural meaning in a particular period, like, "What objects symbolized loyalty in feudal Korea?" or "What items were worn as signs of dissent during the French Revolution?" These little touches say everything without having to explain.

Sometimes, the tension between past and present isn't even within the story—it's between the story and the audience. You might write about a character doing something cruel or ignorant because that's what people did in their time. Maybe your protagonist owns slaves. Maybe they believe women are inferior. Maybe they commit violence for their country or their God without question. The danger here is writing them off as villains or rewriting them to be more palatable. The goal is to let the reader sit with the discomfort. Let them ask, "Would I have believed this too, if I were born in that time?" That's the kind of tension that lingers long after the book is closed or the credits roll.

ChatGPT can help you walk that line by offering nuance. Ask for, "Ways to portray a flawed 19th-century protagonist without modernizing their beliefs," or "How to show a character growing out of a harmful worldview without turning it into a morality lesson." You're not here to judge the past. You're here to *understand* it—and help your readers feel the complexity, not just the clarity.

You can also amplify this tension through plot structure. Try opening your story with something that feels comfortable, noble, or justified—then slowly reveal how that belief or institution was built on something cruel or dishonest. The reader's sense of betrayal mirrors the character's own awakening. Ask ChatGPT to help you structure arcs like this: "Outline a historical drama where a religious leader slowly realizes his teachings are being used to justify political violence," or "Create a plot in which a character discovers their family fortune is tied to exploitation." The tension becomes a slow burn, and every choice the character makes afterward carries more weight.

And if your story does have a modern-day component, you can show the past literally influencing the present. A descendant uncovering letters, a historian questioning records, a survivor telling their story for the first time. Let the ghosts of history shape current conflicts, and let the audience feel how the world we live in was built on foundations that still crack and echo today. ChatGPT can help you braid these timelines together by asking for "ways to connect a present-day narrative with events from the Salem Witch Trials," or "plot devices to link a modern inheritance dispute to land stolen during colonial expansion." The past becomes a force that refuses to stay buried.

In the end, historical drama is never just about what happened. It's about how it *still* happens—in different clothes, in different words, but with the same human need for meaning, identity, and justice. When you create tension between past and present, you're asking the audience to look around their world with new eyes. To feel the weight of tradition. To see how far we've come—and how far we haven't.

Use that tension. Let it crack your characters open. Let it haunt your story's silence. Let it whisper to your reader that nothing ever really dies—not the pain, not the hope, and certainly not the past.

Researching Fast with ChatGPT's Help

If you've ever tried to write historical fiction the old-fashioned way, you know the research process can feel like being buried under an avalanche of books, articles, and contradictory facts. You find yourself swimming through dates, digging through footnotes, and getting stuck for hours on the tiniest of details—what kind of fabric a dress was made of, how long it would take to cross a country by horse, or whether a certain phrase even existed back then. But with ChatGPT, research no longer has to be slow, overwhelming, or disjointed. You can ask smarter questions, get quick answers, and use that momentum to stay in the writing flow. This chapter is all about how to turn ChatGPT into your real-time research partner—keeping your historical drama accurate without grinding your story to a halt.

The first step is knowing how to ask questions that return useful, focused information. Vague queries like "Tell me about 14th-century Europe" will give you too much general background and not enough story fuel. Instead, get hyper-specific. Ask, "What would a merchant's daily routine be like in 14th-century Venice?" or "How were criminals punished in 1300s England?" You're not trying to write a history paper—you're trying to build a believable moment in time that surrounds your characters like a living, breathing world. The sharper your questions, the richer your results.

You can also ask ChatGPT to give you answers in different formats depending on what stage you're in. If you're brainstorming, ask for lists: "Give me ten historical jobs a woman might have had in 18th-century Paris." If you're outlining, ask for summaries: "Summarize the political tensions in Spain during the 1930s." If you're drafting, ask for immersive detail: "Describe the atmosphere in a crowded Roman market around 50 BCE." The flexibility to move between big-picture research and granular texture is one of the biggest advantages of using ChatGPT over a traditional search engine or textbook.

One of the fastest ways to get story-ready material is to treat ChatGPT like a scene consultant. Instead of looking up facts individually, you can build an entire environment in one go. Try something like, "Describe a small village in rural Ireland in 1850, including what the houses look like, what people eat for breakfast, what jobs they do, what kind of music is played, and what clothes children wear." You'll get a compact, vivid starting point with everything you need to write your setting without stopping every few lines to double-check a detail.

Let's say you're writing a confrontation between a nobleman and a servant in 1700s England. You're not sure what kind of power the nobleman legally held over the servant. You could spend half an hour clicking through search results—or you could just ask, "What were the rights and restrictions of household servants in 18th-century England? Could they be dismissed without cause? Could they file complaints?" In less than a minute, you'll know how much authority the nobleman has, how risky the servant's rebellion might be, and what consequences could follow. That's not just helpful. That's story structure delivered on demand.

You can even have ChatGPT help you spot anachronisms before they slip into your draft. Say you write a sentence where a character lights a match in 1600s France. You pause and wonder—were matches even invented yet? Instead of opening a new tab and falling into a Wikipedia rabbit hole, just type, "Did matches exist in 1600s France?" You'll get a direct, clear answer. And if the answer is no, ChatGPT can suggest period-accurate alternatives like flint and steel or fire tongs. These little checks add up to a story that reads as effortlessly authentic.

Sometimes the issue isn't whether something happened, but how people felt about it. That's where ChatGPT really shines. Ask it for emotional or cultural context. Try, "What was the public reaction to female poets in 19th-century

Persia?" or "How did lower-class Germans view the aristocracy in the early 1900s?" Facts are useful, but *feelings* build fiction. You want to know what your characters would believe, fear, admire, or resent based on their culture—and that's something textbooks often don't explain clearly. ChatGPT can bridge that gap.

Another powerful trick is to use ChatGPT to compare time periods or cultures quickly. Suppose you're debating whether to set your story during the Meiji Restoration or the Tokugawa shogunate in Japan. Ask, "What are the key differences between social structures in the Tokugawa era and the Meiji era?" You'll get a clean breakdown of values, politics, class systems, and cultural shifts. You can then choose the version of the past that best fits the story you want to tell. You're no longer researching in a vacuum—you're steering with clarity.

If your story involves war, rebellion, disaster, or political upheaval, you can also use ChatGPT to map out timelines. Ask it, "List the major events in the Irish War of Independence, with dates and locations," or "Give me a day-by-day timeline of the fall of Constantinople." This helps you build your plot around real-world events and align your characters' movements with actual historical rhythms. And if you're writing fiction that runs parallel to a known event, this level of temporal detail will help your story snap into place without ever feeling forced.

One of the best ways to use ChatGPT for research is by testing ideas before you commit. Let's say you have a character who's a spy disguised as a traveling musician in 1500s Spain. Sounds cool, but is it plausible? Ask, "Would it be historically believable for a traveling musician in 1500s Spain to work as a spy? What would make that realistic or unrealistic?" The AI will give you reasons it could work, what challenges that character would face, and how they might communicate covertly. This is how you keep your creativity wild while keeping your feet grounded in truth.

And if you're working on multiple characters from different walks of life—say, a soldier, a baker, a nun, and a pickpocket—ChatGPT can help you build separate cultural profiles for each. Ask, "Describe the daily life of a female baker in Paris during the 1780s," or "What would a Catholic nun believe and practice in 1500s Florence?" You'll be able to jump into each perspective with confidence, layering them together into a complex, believable world.

The beauty of researching with ChatGPT is that it works *with* your writing rhythm, not against it. You don't have to pause for hours or break your flow just to find one accurate detail. You can get what you need quickly, then dive right back into your narrative while the momentum is still fresh. It makes the research process feel less like homework and more like collaboration—because that's exactly what it is. A partnership between your imagination and an always-ready, infinitely curious co-creator.

So don't be afraid to write about unfamiliar eras. Don't hold back your ideas just because you don't know the history—yet. The past is wide open. And with ChatGPT at your fingertips, you can walk through it in real-time, gathering just enough truth to make your fiction sing. You'll research faster, write bolder, and bring the past to life with confidence and style.

Finding the Story Inside the History

History is packed with names, dates, battles, treaties, plagues, revolutions, and royal bloodlines. It's a maze of facts and figures—but historical drama isn't about that. It's about people. It's about human moments hidden between the lines of textbooks. The goal is not to teach history—it's to reveal the emotional truth behind it. So when you sit down to write, you're not just looking for a period to explore or a famous event to retell. You're digging through the grand noise of the past to find the story inside it—the quiet, sharp, personal drama that turns history into narrative. That's the moment it becomes art. And that's exactly what we're doing in this chapter.

The trick is learning how to read between the lines of historical records. That battle? Someone died in someone else's arms. That treaty? It shattered a family legacy. That law? It ruined a love affair. Every major event in history happened to someone who never made it into the books. And your job, as the writer, is to imagine their story. The best historical fiction doesn't invent the world—it discovers the people living just outside the spotlight and pulls them forward. You find the emotion beneath the record. The heartbreak inside the headline.

You can start by picking a historical event or era that interests you—something with stakes, transformation, or cultural friction. Then ask yourself, who was affected in a way that didn't make it into the footnotes? You can use ChatGPT to brainstorm characters who might have been on the fringes of a big event. Ask, "Who might have been affected by the Spanish Inquisition but never mentioned in the records?" or "Create three fictional characters who would have lived through the construction of the Great Wall of China." These are your entry points—characters who give you a human-scale lens to view the larger world.

Sometimes the story is hidden inside a moment of contradiction. A man who benefits from an oppressive system but starts questioning it. A soldier who wins a war but loses everything that mattered. A queen who holds power but not freedom. These contradictions create characters who carry emotional conflict—and emotional conflict is where your plot lives. Ask ChatGPT for examples of social, political, or moral contradictions within a time period. Try prompts like, "What hypocrisies existed in the French aristocracy before the Revolution?" or "What contradictions would a devout Christian slaveholder in the American South struggle with?" These tensions become the skeleton of your narrative arc.

You can also uncover story by zeroing in on transitional periods—eras when the world was shifting beneath people's feet. These are historical goldmines. Think of the fall of empires, the rise of religions, the spread of diseases, or the beginning of industrialization. Ask ChatGPT, "What major cultural shifts were happening in 10th-century Baghdad?" or "What did people fear and hope for during the Enlightenment?" Those hopes and fears are the heartbeat of great drama. They allow you to build characters who are trying to hold on to something as the world changes around them—or trying to change the world before it crushes them.

Another way to find the story inside history is to focus on decisions. Big, risky, world-changing decisions. Not the ones made by kings and generals, but by ordinary people caught in the crossfire. The decision to run. To stay. To lie. To fight. To betray. History is full of those forks in the road. You can build an entire story around a single moment where a character makes a choice that changes the course of their life. Ask ChatGPT, "What moral dilemmas might a nurse face during the Crimean War?" or "What difficult choices would a Jewish family confront in 1930s Germany?" That's your story—not the war or the law or the headline—but the choice.

Sometimes, you'll find your story by following the money. Economics often reveal what people truly value, fear, or fight over. Ask ChatGPT to explain the economic pressures in a particular period: "What financial hardships did peasants face in feudal Japan?" or "What kind of wealth disparity existed in pre-revolutionary Haiti?" Once you know who has money, who needs it, and what people are willing to do to get it—you've got drama, conflict, and motivation ready to go.

You can also find your story by looking at what was forbidden. Wherever there were taboos, there were people breaking them. Lovers, thinkers, rebels, artists, dissidents—this is where some of the most compelling characters come from. Ask ChatGPT, "What kinds of behaviors were forbidden for women in ancient Rome?" or "What beliefs were considered dangerous during the Protestant Reformation?" These cultural walls are your invitation to write the people who tried to climb over them—or were crushed underneath them.

Don't forget the small, domestic moments, either. History isn't just politics and war. It's childbirth, hunger, heartbreak, jealousy, friendship, regret. A woman waiting for a husband who never returns from sea. A boy who watches his family's farm be swallowed by a tax debt. A servant who falls in love with the master's son. These aren't world-changing events on the surface—but they're everything to the people living them. Ask ChatGPT for small-scale stories inside big moments. "Describe the daily life of a widow during the Irish Famine." "What private struggles might a teacher have faced during the Cultural Revolution in China?" These quieter dramas often hit harder than any war scene ever could.

If you already know the kind of emotional journey you want to write—a story of forgiveness, betrayal, loss, rebellion, or transformation—you can reverse engineer the setting by asking, "What historical periods would naturally create a story about [insert emotional theme]?" For example, a story about trust and betrayal could play beautifully in the Cold War. A story about ambition and downfall might fit in the fading days of the Roman Empire. Let ChatGPT help you pair theme with historical setting, and you'll find a story that grows organically out of its time.

Finding the story inside the history is not about rewriting the past. It's about pulling back the curtain on everything the records didn't capture. You're not interested in telling what happened. You're interested in how it felt. Who it destroyed. Who it transformed. Who it quietly saved. And those stories are everywhere—hiding in the shadows, waiting for someone to tell them with heart.

So the next time you feel overwhelmed by dates and battles and treaties, remember: that's just the scaffolding. The real story lives in the cracks. Ask better questions. Follow the human thread. Use ChatGPT to help you peel away the surface. And watch the past become a stage where your characters can finally step into the light.

Plotting a Historical Drama from Climax to Origin

Most people are taught to build a story from the beginning—start with a character's childhood, build the world around them, and let things unfold chronologically. But historical drama isn't always best served by a straight line. When history is already full of tension and consequence, it can be far more powerful to write backward—to start with the climax and then work in reverse to discover how everything fell into place. When you reverse-engineer your story like this, every scene earns its place, and every moment is infused with meaning. You're not just telling what happened. You're telling why it *had* to happen.

Starting from the climax means choosing the emotional and narrative high point first. This isn't just the biggest event—it's the moment where your protagonist is broken, redeemed, transformed, or destroyed. It's where everything that matters finally crashes into them. In historical drama, the climax is often tied to real events: a battle, an execution, an escape, a betrayal. But it can also be intimate—a personal confession, a lost love, a final act of courage in the face of silence. The key is that it represents the emotional truth of your story.

Ask ChatGPT to help you brainstorm powerful climactic moments grounded in historical contexts. Try, "Give me examples of emotional climaxes set during the Salem witch trials," or "Suggest a final turning point for a female spy in Nazi-occupied France." Choose the moment that strikes a nerve. If it gives you goose-bumps or makes you whisper "yes, that's it," you've found your ending.

Once your climax is clear, work backward and ask: what kind of character would end up here? Not what kind of character could—but what kind of character *must*. What fears, flaws, beliefs, or loyalties would lead them to this moment? If your climax is a soldier disobeying a direct order to save civilians, then maybe earlier he was a rule-follower who always obeyed authority. If your climax is a queen sacrificing her throne to protect a forbidden child, maybe earlier she believed power was the only thing that mattered. The distance between who they were and who they become is your story.

You can use ChatGPT to build that arc. Ask, "What emotional journey might lead a loyal knight to betray his king during a religious crusade?" or "What kind of upbringing would cause a peasant girl to rise as a revolutionary leader?" These aren't just backstory prompts—they're structure tools. They show you the steps you need to reveal, in reverse, as you build back to the origin.

Each scene from the climax backward should serve one purpose: to explain how we got here. Not in exposition—but in emotion. If your character betrays a friend in the climax, we should see earlier moments of doubt, silence, compromise. If your character leads a charge into battle, we should see when they were afraid, unsure, lost. You're planting the seeds of the climax, but in reverse. That structure keeps every chapter focused and purposeful.

Let's say your historical drama ends with a woman standing alone at a dock, watching a ship leave, knowing she's just let go of the only man she's ever loved to save his life. That's your climax. What scene comes just before that? Maybe it's the argument where she convinces him to go. Before that? Maybe she risks everything to forge documents for him. Before that? She's learning what fate awaits him if he stays. Before that? She's still loyal to the state and wouldn't dream of helping a traitor. And even further back? She's just an obedient wife, going through the motions.

You're not just mapping plot points—you're building emotional erosion. Layer by layer, you show how each compromise, discovery, or act of courage reshapes the protagonist. And because you know the ending, you won't get lost in subplots that don't matter. Everything bends toward the final moment.

If you hit a wall and can't figure out how a character could make such a massive leap—from innocent to assassin, from coward to rebel—ChatGPT can help you fill in the cracks. Ask, "What emotional events would push a loyal government worker to help an outlaw escape?" or "Give me a believable path from royal tutor to revolutionary executioner." Let the AI propose bridges between psychological points. Use the ones that resonate and discard the rest. But every suggestion will move you closer to a structure that feels inevitable.

Another advantage of plotting backward is that it creates natural tension for the reader or viewer. They know from the beginning that something big is coming. Maybe you even open on the climax, then jump back in time. That's a classic storytelling technique in screenwriting and novels alike. The audience is hooked not by wondering *what* happens, but *how*. That's a deeper kind of suspense—emotional, layered, and mature. You're giving them a puzzle to solve, one scene at a time.

You can even ask ChatGPT to map your entire story for you. Try, "Plot a three-act historical drama that starts with a climactic betrayal and works backward to reveal how it happened." You'll get a blueprint with major beats, reversals, and developments. Then you can customize it with your own characters, style, and subplots. It's like having a flexible outline ready to evolve as you write.

Reverse plotting also helps you decide when to reveal information. Historical drama often involves secrets—affairs, hidden loyalties, forbidden knowledge. When you start with the climax, you can time your reveals to add maximum impact. You can ask ChatGPT to suggest when to reveal key events: "When should the audience learn the protagonist is spying for the enemy if the climax is his execution?" Structure becomes strategy.

As you work backward to the origin, your final scene (which will be the story's first chronologically) should feel inevitable but surprising. It's the moment when the character's life was still unbroken. Maybe they believe in the system. Maybe they're innocent. Maybe they're asleep inside a life that will soon demand everything from them. That quiet beginning becomes a loaded opening once you've seen where it all ends. And when the reader finally returns to that moment in memory, it hits harder than it ever could have at the start.

Plotting a historical drama from climax to origin isn't just a structural trick—it's a way of writing with intention. You build tension from knowledge. You sculpt character from transformation. And you make every moment matter, because you've seen where it's all going. With ChatGPT helping you connect the dots, you can move quickly, test bold directions, and craft a story that feels deliberate, layered, and unforgettable.

Because when you write backward, you're not just telling what happened. You're revealing why it *had* to. And that's what makes historical drama not only powerful—but timeless.

The Three-Act Structure in Historical Drama

Historical drama might take place in ancient ruins, candlelit castles, or the blood-soaked alleys of a revolution, but at its heart, it runs on the same engine that drives all great storytelling: structure. And while historical settings add complexity, beauty, and context, the three-act structure keeps your story tight, emotional, and purposeful. It's the framework that turns scattered facts into a gripping arc. It ensures that your story—whether set in feudal Japan or Renaissance Italy—doesn't just wander through time but builds toward something that matters.

Let's break it down in a way that makes it feel usable. In a historical drama, Act One is the world as it was. Act Two is the disruption of that world. Act Three is the cost of that disruption—and what, if anything, is reborn from it. The beauty of the three-act structure is that it fits naturally with the way history moves: calm, crisis, and consequence.

Start with Act One. This is where you set the stage—not just the literal setting, but the ideological setting. What does your protagonist believe? What does the world around them demand of them? What roles are they playing to survive in this time and place? This act introduces not only your character, but the pressures of their historical world. Maybe your protagonist is a young woman in 18th-century China being groomed for an arranged marriage. She believes obedience is survival. Or maybe your story begins in Berlin during the rise of Nazism, and your lead is a schoolteacher who believes politics have no place in the classroom. This is your chance to lay down the moral landscape before anything shakes it.

You don't need to stuff Act One with too much history—just enough to feel grounded. Ask ChatGPT to help with this. Try, "What would the daily life of a lower-class woman in 18th-century China look like?" or "What were the cultural pressures on German schoolteachers in the early 1930s?" These details will let your Act One breathe without bogging it down in exposition. You want the reader to understand what *normal* looks like in this world, because that's what will soon be disrupted.

Then you move into Act Two—the confrontation. This is where something changes. Something shifts. Something breaks. It could be personal, political, emotional, or literal. In historical drama, Act Two is often when your protagonist begins to see that the system they live in is unjust or fragile or poisoned at its core. That arranged marriage? It's to a man twice her age who sees her as a tool. That schoolteacher? He's asked to report students who question the state. Suddenly, the world isn't what it seemed, and your protagonist has to act—even if that action is hesitant, clumsy, or doomed.

Act Two is about pressure. Social, internal, external. It's where your protagonist is pulled in two directions: loyalty to the world they know, or allegiance to what they're starting to feel is right. ChatGPT can help you craft these crises by asking, "What social punishments would a woman face for defying her family in 18th-century China?" or "What dangers would a teacher face for resisting Nazi propaganda?" Use these answers to raise the stakes. Let every scene tighten the emotional noose around your character's neck. This is the act where readers lean in. It's where your character's beliefs crack, where allies become enemies, and where the historical backdrop roars to life.

This act often ends in collapse. The protagonist either acts and fails, or doesn't act and faces the consequences. Either way, things fall apart. Maybe the marriage goes through and your heroine is silenced. Maybe the teacher is arrested. Maybe a revolution begins and everything spirals into violence. Act Two ends with a question: Can anything be saved? That question is what pushes us into the final stretch.

Then comes Act Three—the resolution. This is where your protagonist either rises or falls. And it has to cost them something. In historical drama, Act Three is often tragic, or at least bittersweet. Because history doesn't always end in justice. But it should end in meaning. Your character might die, but they die changed. Or they survive, but the world they knew is gone. The woman who was married off becomes the secret voice behind a rebellion. The teacher is exiled but helps others resist from afar. These outcomes should reflect the emotional journey more than the historical accuracy. You're telling a story with history—not bound to it.

Act Three also needs to show the full force of the historical world reacting to the protagonist's choices. This isn't just about wrapping up a plot. It's about revealing the full moral cost of the time period. Let ChatGPT help you forecast this by asking, "What legal or cultural consequences would a female rebel face in 18th-century China?" or "What would happen to a political dissenter under the Third Reich after being discovered?" These answers shape the emotional realism of your final scenes. Whether your ending is triumphant or devastating, it should feel inevitable.

Throughout all three acts, structure isn't about restricting your creativity—it's about giving it form. It lets you balance big historical moments with intimate emotional beats. It keeps you from wandering off course or losing momentum. And when you know where you are in the three-act flow, you can always recalibrate your scenes. Ask yourself: Does this scene reveal something about the protagonist's belief system? Does it move them closer to change or deeper into conflict? Does it build toward the climax, or pull away from it?

You can also use ChatGPT to outline your entire arc from the top. Try a prompt like, "Create a three-act structure for a historical drama about a Black journalist in 1920s Harlem uncovering police corruption." You'll get a full narrative flow: a world of jazz and silence in Act One, growing threats and ethical dilemmas in Act Two, and a final reckoning in Act Three. You can use this structure as a spine to build your own character, setting, and themes around.

Historical drama thrives when the personal and the political collide—and the three-act structure is your blueprint for staging that collision. It gives you a path, but also space to detour, deepen, and dramatize. It's a rhythm older than any time period you could write about. And when you work with it, not against it, your story takes on a shape that just feels right—even when everything inside it is falling apart.

So whether you're writing about a revolution, a forbidden love, a war, or a quiet moment of defiance in a forgotten century, trust the three-act structure to hold the weight of your vision. Let it carry your characters through the storm, and let the past rise up in every beat. Because history, after all, is nothing but one long, aching act of conflict—and drama is how we make sense of it.

How to Use Conflict to Reflect the Era's Struggles

Conflict is the heartbeat of drama, but in historical storytelling, it does something even more powerful—it acts as a lens. Through your character's struggles, arguments, betrayals, and moral battles, the audience comes to understand not just the individual story but the entire world that shaped it. Conflict in historical drama is never isolated. It echoes the social systems, cultural pressures, political unrest, religious laws, and economic divisions of the time. In other words, when your characters fight, it's not just personal—it's historical. It's your chance to dramatize what the era itself was fighting over.

So how do you build conflict that reflects the era instead of just happening inside it? You begin with the questions the time period was already asking. Was it a time of religious intolerance? Patriarchal dominance? Class stratification? Slavery? Colonization? Censorship? These historical forces didn't just shape nations—they shaped how individuals thought, loved, obeyed, and resisted. When you embed those forces into your conflict, your story gains layers that no amount of costumes or period detail can offer.

Let's say you're writing a story set during the British Empire's colonization of India. It's tempting to write a love story between a British officer and an Indian woman as if it's just forbidden romance. But to reflect the era's struggles, you have to push deeper. What does that romance say about power, identity, shame, and resistance? What internalized values are each character carrying? Does the Indian woman fear social exile? Does the British officer believe in the superiority of his culture, even as he loves someone outside it? Now the conflict isn't just love vs. society—it's colonialism vs. humanity, dominance vs. vulnerability. That's how you turn a personal conflict into a historical one.

You can use ChatGPT to help frame these deeper tensions by asking, "What cultural, political, or economic conflicts defined 19th-century British-ruled India?" or "How might a relationship across class and race lines be received in colonial society?" The more specific your questions, the more revealing the answers. These insights will help you build character motivations that are grounded in their world and not just modern interpretations of right and wrong.

One of the strongest ways to reflect historical struggle is through internal conflict. Think of a priest in Inquisition-era Spain who begins to doubt the church's authority. He's not just struggling with faith—he's struggling with the entire power structure of his world. His doubt threatens his survival, his identity, and his place in the divine order. Or consider a woman in 1950s America torn between her role as a housewife and her desire to work. Her longing is political, even if she doesn't know it. It's a conflict of gender roles, economics, and post-war expectations. You can ask ChatGPT, "What were the emotional and social risks of defying gender norms in 1950s America?" or "What would a priest risk by questioning the church's authority in 16th-century Spain?" Now the internal struggle becomes a thread in the era's larger tapestry.

Family conflict is another rich area. A son who wants to join a revolution while his father clings to tradition. A daughter who refuses a marriage arranged to secure land or peace. A sibling who chooses loyalty to the throne over loyalty to blood. These storylines don't exist in a vacuum—they're dramatizing generational friction, political upheaval, shifting values. Ask ChatGPT, "What would cause conflict between generations in a samurai family during the Meiji Restoration?" or "How did industrialization create family tensions in 19th-century England?" These conflicts humanize massive historical changes.

Class conflict is especially potent in historical drama. Wealth disparity has always shaped opportunity, marriage, education, and even the right to speak freely. When a lower-class character challenges someone above them, it's not just about pride or revenge—it's a threat to the social order. Imagine a butler in Victorian England who exposes a scandal in the household. He's not just acting for justice—he's crossing a boundary enforced by generations of etiquette and control. You can ask ChatGPT, "What would happen to a servant who defied their employer in 19th-century Britain?" or "What kind of tensions existed between merchants and aristocrats in feudal France?" The answers will help you write conflict that's layered with meaning.

Religious and philosophical conflict is also central to many time periods. Think of the Protestant Reformation, the Enlightenment, the Crusades, the rise of communism. These were moments when ideas themselves were dangerous. Writing a character who questions doctrine in the wrong time can be a death sentence—or a revolutionary spark. And even if your story is more intimate, a single prayer, a whispered doubt, or a hidden book can become a symbol of larger unrest. Ask ChatGPT to help create tension in this area: "How were religious heresies punished in 15th-century Italy?" or "What philosophical debates were happening in 18th-century France during the Enlightenment?" Let those tensions shape your character arcs.

Sometimes, the conflict comes from survival. Hunger, war, disease, law. If you're writing about plague-era Europe, your conflict might not be rebellion—it might be whether your character steals bread or starves. But even this kind of conflict reflects the era's structure: who gets to live, who's left behind, what systems collapse under pressure. It's about more than physical need—it's about the human cost of historical conditions. Ask ChatGPT to guide these stakes: "How did famine affect family dynamics during the Irish Potato Famine?" or "What legal punishments existed for theft during the Black Death in England?"

And don't forget, conflict doesn't have to be loud. It can be a silent refusal, a dangerous thought, a letter never sent. In repressive times, the quietest act can be the most radical. A woman who doesn't kneel. A man who walks out of a speech. A child who lies about their name. These small acts of resistance say everything about the world they're trying to survive in. Ask ChatGPT, "What quiet forms of protest existed in authoritarian regimes?" or "How could a person resist oppression without speaking?" You'll find tension where you least expect it.

In the end, conflict in historical drama isn't just a story device. It's a magnifying glass. It shows us what people cared about, feared, and bled for. It makes the past feel immediate. And when it's done well, it makes the audience ask questions—not just about the world back then, but about the one they live in now.

So don't settle for conflict that could happen in any era. Let the era itself *be* the conflict. Let every clash, argument, or act of defiance echo the systems that ruled your characters' lives. Use ChatGPT to dig into the beliefs, laws, customs, and contradictions of the time. Then channel all of it into drama that pulses with historical truth.

Because the more honest your conflict is to the era, the more timeless your story will become.

Letting Themes Shape Your Story's Soul

In historical drama, it's easy to get caught up in the details—the dusty boots, the candlelit corridors, the timelines, the dialects, the weather on the day of the execution. These details matter, but they aren't the soul of your story. The soul lives in your theme. It's the emotional current running beneath every scene. It's the question your story keeps asking, whether whispered or screamed, again and again. It's what stays with the audience long after they've turned the final page or watched the last frame. When you let your theme shape your story's soul, you're not just writing about the past—you're writing through it, straight into the heart of now.

A theme is not a slogan or a message. It's not a moral. It's a conversation between your characters and their world, between their beliefs and the consequences of those beliefs. It's abstract, yes, but it gets expressed through action, conflict, and transformation. A theme could be the cost of silence, the danger of loyalty, the burden of legacy, or the slow erosion of innocence. It's something you feel rather than state. And in historical drama, it becomes especially potent because history itself is built on thematic contradictions—freedom versus control, tradition versus change, love versus law.

So how do you find your theme? Start by asking what haunts you about the time period you're writing. What makes you angry, inspired, broken, or amazed? Is it the way women were treated? The lies people told to protect their kingdoms? The quiet rebellions that no one ever wrote down? Whatever stirs your gut—that's your theme trying to speak. You can use ChatGPT to help uncover these ideas. Ask, "What thematic questions arise from writing about women during the Salem witch trials?" or "What emotional themes are tied to stories about soldiers in World War I?" Let those answers simmer. The right theme will give your story purpose.

Once you have a sense of your theme, let it influence every part of your storytelling. Characters aren't just people with goals—they're expressions of the theme in motion. If your story is about freedom, then each character should have a different relationship to it. One clings to it. One fears it. One dies for it. One doesn't even believe it's possible. This variety creates narrative depth. It allows you to explore your theme from multiple emotional angles.

Take a story set in Stalinist Russia with a theme of "truth versus survival." Your protagonist might be a poet who writes propaganda to protect their family. Another character might be a neighbor who reports people for personal gain. Another might be a prisoner who refuses to speak at all. Each of these characters reveals a different way of dealing with truth under pressure. The theme becomes a thread, pulling through each life, showing how the system shapes—or crushes—them.

ChatGPT can help you build a cast around your theme. Try a prompt like, "Create a group of characters who each represent different emotional responses to the theme of silence in a repressive society." The result will give you a cast of perspectives, not just plot functions. And when each character's conflict is a reflection of the central theme, your story gains cohesion. It becomes something more than a sequence of events—it becomes an exploration.

Setting, too, becomes a tool of theme. Think of the environment as a character that reinforces what your story is really about. If your theme is about isolation, maybe the story takes place in a remote lighthouse town during a war. If it's about change, set it in a city being rapidly industrialized, with buildings going up and traditions being torn down. ChatGPT can offer ideas here as well. Ask, "What historical locations reflect the theme of lost identity?" or "Suggest settings that evoke the theme of transformation during the Renaissance." You're not just choosing where your story takes place. You're choosing the emotional architecture of the story itself.

Your theme also helps guide pacing. A story about rage and revolution might move fast, brutal, and chaotic—mirroring the emotional storm of the characters. A story about grief, memory, or shame might be slower, more reflective, full of silences and unresolved moments. Think of theme as the story's pulse. Let it set the rhythm. Ask ChatGPT, "How does the theme of regret affect narrative pacing?" or "What story beats support a theme of suppressed desire in historical drama?" Let the emotional logic drive the structure, not just the historical facts.

Dialogue becomes more meaningful when it echoes your theme, not through repetition but through emotional pressure. The things characters argue about, hide from, or fail to say are usually tied to the story's central question. If your theme is about the cost of ambition, maybe two brothers speak in cold, transactional terms until one finally breaks. If your theme is redemption, maybe the most powerful line is the one never spoken—because the character can't forgive themselves. You can ask ChatGPT to help shape dialogue that mirrors emotional themes: "Write a conversation between two lovers in 1930s Germany where they argue over loyalty and fear," or "Give me a monologue that explores the theme of honor in a crumbling samurai household."

Even plot twists gain more power when they're in conversation with your theme. The best surprises in historical drama aren't just shocking—they're thematically loaded. A character who's been seeking justice discovers they've been complicit in injustice all along. A lover who seemed faithful turns out to have sacrificed everything behind the scenes. These twists hit harder because they challenge what the story has led us to believe. ChatGPT can help you brainstorm twists tied to theme by asking, "What plot reveals could deepen a theme about self-deception in a Victorian setting?" or "Suggest betrayals that connect with a theme about power and control in ancient Rome."

And finally, your ending. The theme should crystallize in that final moment, not through exposition or a lesson, but through change. Your protagonist doesn't need to win—but they need to evolve. If your story is about truth, maybe they finally speak it, no matter the cost. If it's about love in a world that forbids it, maybe they choose it, even if they lose everything. The ending is where the soul of the story comes into full light. ChatGPT can help guide this too: "How should a story about forgiveness end if set during the Rwandan Genocide?" or "What would a thematically consistent ending be for a character struggling with loyalty in Tudor England?"

Letting your theme shape your story's soul doesn't mean being preachy or obvious. It means writing with a kind of emotional compass. A sense that underneath the plot and costumes and language, something deeper is being worked out. Something that touches both the time you're writing about—and the time we're living in now.

Because themes don't just help you write better stories. They help you ask better questions. And in historical drama, the best stories are the ones that take something ancient and make it feel urgently, heartbreakingly present. That's what a theme does when you let it lead. It turns memory into meaning. And it gives your story a soul worth remembering.

Creating Settings That Feel Alive

A historical drama lives or dies on the strength of its setting. You could write a masterpiece of character and dialogue, but if the world feels flat—if it's just a backdrop painted with historical facts—your story loses its magic. The setting in a historical drama isn't just a place where things happen. It's a force. It breathes, it shapes behavior, it feeds conflict, and it influences mood. When it's done right, the setting doesn't just feel alive—it feels like a character itself. And bringing it to life isn't about dumping period facts onto the page. It's about evoking a time, a culture, and a mood that envelops the reader or viewer so completely, they forget they're not really there.

So how do you do that? You don't start with geography or architecture. You start with *feeling*. Ask yourself, what do I want the audience to *feel* in this world? Is it oppression? Grandeur? Chaos? Loneliness? Decay? Hope? That emotional core will guide the sensory details you choose to include. A bustling 19th-century Cairo marketplace filled with heat, spice, noise, and movement creates a different feeling than a cold, silent monastery in 12th-century Ireland where every sound is sacred. Each setting tells a story—yours just needs to tell the right one.

Use ChatGPT to help brainstorm immersive sensory palettes for different periods and places. Ask, "Describe the textures, sounds, and smells of a rural Russian village in the winter of 1890," or "What does a courtroom in 15th-century Florence feel like during a public trial?" You're not looking for a textbook answer—you're looking for language that evokes atmosphere, that gives you a feeling to build on.

Details matter, but it's not about cramming every historical fact you can find into one paragraph. It's about choosing the right details—the ones that reveal culture, emotion, and hierarchy. Instead of saying "the castle was huge," show the drafty corridors, the rusting armor by the fireplace, the smoke-stained tapestries that haven't been replaced in a generation. Instead of saying "the city was in crisis," let the reader hear the bells ringing for curfew, see the boarded windows, and feel the tension in the way people avoid eye contact in the streets. The more you anchor your descriptions in character perspective, the more alive the setting becomes.

One of the most powerful techniques for building a living setting is to show how people *use* their environment. How do they dress to survive it? How do they modify it to fit their needs? What do they believe about the land, the weather, the city, the ruins nearby? A dying forest might be a place of fear or sacred power. A palace might look grand from a distance but feel like a prison to the servant cleaning its stone floors. Let your characters interact with the world, not just pass through it. Ask ChatGPT for examples like, "How would a medieval peasant interact with their home and surroundings on a daily basis?" or "What signs of weather and terrain would a soldier in ancient Greece look for when choosing a camp location?"

Setting is also an opportunity to layer in theme. If your story is about decay, maybe everything around your characters is crumbling—buildings, ideals, relationships. If it's about oppression, maybe even the architecture reinforces it: doors too narrow, windows too high, guards posted in sight at all times. If your theme is beauty under pressure, your setting might contrast natural wonder with human cruelty—a garden blooming inside a prison yard. You can ask ChatGPT to help you design locations based on theme: "Design a city layout that reflects a society obsessed with class structure," or "Create a village where everything is beautiful on the surface but hiding something dark."

Another often overlooked aspect of setting is *change*. Real historical worlds weren't static. Towns expanded. Empires collapsed. Plagues swept through. Floods destroyed farms. New technologies disrupted old ways. When your setting evolves, it adds tension and realism. Show how your characters react to those changes. A printing press arrives, and suddenly the monks feel obsolete. A new road is built, and the town becomes a trading hub overnight. Ask ChatGPT, "What technologies reshaped everyday life in 17th-century France?" or "How did industrialization transform small towns in early 1800s England?" Let your setting move with the story.

Dialogue can also be used to reinforce setting. The way people speak, the metaphors they use, the assumptions baked into their language—all reflect the world they live in. A sailor from the 1700s might speak in superstitions and navigation terms. A nobleman from 16th-century Florence might speak with legal precision or religious references. Let your characters speak like products of their environment. Use ChatGPT to shape voices: "What kind of slang would a Victorian pickpocket use?" or "Write dialogue between two farmers in 1930s Oklahoma during a dust storm." You're building voice through world.

Don't forget about class and power. Who controls the space? Who fears it? Who's allowed where, and who isn't? A marketplace isn't the same place for a merchant as it is for a thief. A church isn't the same for a nobleman as it is for a heretic. Settings aren't neutral—they're shaped by power dynamics, and they shape character experience in return. Use ChatGPT to explore, "How was social status reflected in home layouts during the Ottoman Empire?" or "What areas were forbidden to lower-class citizens in Ancient Rome?"

Even weather can carry emotional weight. Rain during a funeral doesn't just add atmosphere—it can echo the story's grief. A sudden heatwave in a tense city can make tempers boil. A snowstorm can isolate your characters just when they most need help. Let the environment reflect the inner world of your characters. It makes the drama deeper and more immersive.

In historical drama, your setting should never feel like an exhibit in a museum. It should be lived in. Dirty. Lively. Flawed. Full of smells, sounds, secrets, and contradictions. People should eat in it, cry in it, hide in it, hope in it. It should be a place that could break them—or change them—just by being real.

So when you're creating your setting, don't think like a historian. Think like a time traveler. Step inside. Run your hand over the wall. Close your eyes and listen. Then open them, and start writing. Let ChatGPT fill in the blanks, answer the strange questions, and help you paint the corners of the world you didn't even know were there.

Because once your setting feels alive, your story no longer reads like fiction. It feels like memory—someone's real, aching, unforgettable memory—and that's what makes historical drama sing.

The Sounds, Smells, and Sights of a Lost World

Historical drama isn't just a genre—it's an invitation to walk through the past with all five senses wide open. You can have compelling characters, sharp dialogue, and a tight plot, but if the world doesn't feel sensory, it won't feel real. What makes a historical world come alive isn't just what happens in it—it's the *experience* of being there. And that experience is built through sound, smell, and sight—the unspoken language of immersion.

When you write about a "lost world," you're not just reconstructing it from facts. You're resurrecting its heartbeat. You're trying to understand what it felt like to live in that time, not just know what occurred. That heartbeat isn't found in textbooks—it's found in the sound of hooves on cobblestone at dawn, in the stink of chamber pots dumped into alleyways, in the color of bruised peaches rotting on a merchant's stall. It's not about overwhelming your reader with information—it's about creating an atmosphere so vivid, they forget they're reading and start breathing the air of another century.

The first place to start is with **sound**. Every time period had its own soundtrack, and it rarely involved silence. A 14th-century city buzzed with street vendors yelling over one another, dogs barking, blacksmiths hammering, the clatter of wooden wheels, and church bells marking time. Compare that to a nomadic tribe on the Mongolian steppes—wind whistling across plains, the lowing of livestock, guttural singing over the fire. Or a 1920s jazz club in Harlem—the clink of glasses, syncopated rhythms, the hum of secrets exchanged between dances. Think about what your world sounds like during its quietest moments and its loudest. Ask ChatGPT, "What would a port city in 17th-century Japan sound like at night?" or "What noises would fill a battlefield camp the night before combat in ancient Greece?" Let those answers guide the soundscape of your scenes.

Next, move to **smell**, the most emotionally evocative sense. It's often overlooked, but nothing connects a reader to a world faster than scent. Smell carries memory. A character walking through a spice market in Marrakesh in the 1500s will remember more than just what they saw—they'll carry the sting of saffron, the sweetness of dried rose petals, and the sweat of the crowd pressing in. Or take a London street in the 1800s: the smell of coal smoke, rain on soot-stained cobblestone, and the sour stench of rotting refuse left in alleyways. Smell builds realism, but more importantly, it builds *emotion*. Ask ChatGPT for help like, "What smells would a medieval healer's hut be filled with?" or "Describe the scents that might overwhelm a Roman banquet." You'll find your characters' emotions shifting with every inhalation.

Then comes **sight**, the most expected but also the most layered. Historical worlds often had a visual hierarchy. Colors meant status. Clothing showed allegiance. Weapons were ceremonial as well as deadly. Even architecture carried power—tall ceilings to intimidate, small windows to control light and mood. What did people *see* every day that shaped how they felt? A peasant might see cracked hands and harvest stains. A monk might see illuminated texts and candle wax puddled on stone. A child in wartime might see uniforms and disappearances. Ask ChatGPT, "What colors and designs were popular among aristocrats in 18th-century France?" or "What would a rural Chinese village look like after a heavy monsoon in the 1600s?" Don't just describe scenery—use sight to tell the story of survival, fear, beauty, or decay.

To bring it all together, consider how all three senses operate at once in any given scene. Let's say your story is set in a plague-stricken city. Don't just write that the streets are empty. Let the reader hear the buzzing of flies around boarded doors, smell the acrid lime thrown on bodies, and see the way neighbors peek from shuttered windows like ghosts. Or maybe your character is riding through the countryside after a lost battle. The sounds of distant wolves echo across the hills. The air smells of wet leather and burnt wood. The sky is the color of bruises. The sensory world becomes a reflection of inner turmoil.

Don't limit these sensations to description, either—let them influence *action*. If a character smells smoke, they go investigate. If they hear footsteps behind them in a darkened hallway, they hold their breath. If they see a banner with a rival family crest, they feel rage boil in their stomach. The sensory world should provoke choices, not just paint pictures.

And remember, the senses don't always tell the truth. They can distort. The same sound might be calming or terrifying depending on context. A perfume might trigger longing in one moment and grief in the next. Let your characters misread the world through their senses, especially when under pressure. This creates dramatic irony, tension, and emotional depth.

If you're feeling stuck or unsure how to enrich a scene, ask ChatGPT to generate immersive sensory snapshots. Try, "Describe the sensory experience of walking through a temple in ancient Egypt at dusk," or "Create a vivid scene using all five senses in a 1930s Italian coastal town." Let the AI give you something textured, then reshape it to suit your characters and tone.

And finally, don't feel like you need to include all senses in every paragraph. A little goes a long way. The right sound at the right moment—a whip cracking, a door creaking, a crowd gasping—can be more powerful than a page of exposition. A single smell can evoke an entire childhood. A flash of red silk or blood can stop time. You're not writing a documentary. You're writing an emotional memory of a world that once was.

So step into your setting. Smell the smoke. Hear the bells. Look at the sky through eyes that have never seen electricity or heard an airplane. Use ChatGPT to help you build the skeleton of history—and then you, the writer, breathe life into it with every sensory brushstroke.

Because the sounds, smells, and sights of a lost world are more than just atmosphere—they're the soul of the past whispering, *I was here.* And your job is to make the reader feel it.

Writing Dialogue That Feels Authentic Without Being Clunky

Dialogue in historical drama is one of those tightropes every writer must walk. On one side, there's the risk of making your characters sound like modern people in fancy costumes, tossing out contemporary idioms in corsets or chainmail. On the other side, there's the danger of drowning your scenes in stilted, overly formal, or archaic language that may be accurate—but also unreadable. The sweet spot is somewhere in between: dialogue that feels true to the era, emotionally believable, and—most importantly—*clear*. You want your characters to sound like they belong to their time without making the reader feel like they've been assigned a Shakespearean monologue at a school assembly.

So how do you strike that balance? First, understand this: authenticity in dialogue isn't about exact replication of historical speech. It's about *illusion*. You're not writing a linguistic museum piece. You're crafting something that *feels* period-appropriate, even if the words aren't lifted from old letters or records. Think of it like a film set—it may not be a real castle, but the way it's lit, dressed, and filmed convinces us it is. Dialogue works the same way. It should echo the tone, rhythm, and values of the era without losing the reader in a sea of "thees," "thous," and obscure idioms.

Start with rhythm and word choice. Historical characters often spoke more formally than we do today, especially in public or official settings, but they still had personalities, habits, and emotional quirks. A nobleman from the 18th century might speak with polished diction, but he'd still get impatient or flustered. A servant might use simpler language, but that doesn't mean they speak in clichés. Use ChatGPT to test speech patterns: "Write a conversation between a 1700s French noblewoman and her maid, showing class difference through dialogue," or "Give me a natural-sounding disagreement between two Roman senators." You'll get a structure you can adapt and simplify as needed.

Next, remember that context defines tone. In many historical settings, people didn't speak as freely as we do now—especially across class, gender, or religious lines. A servant would often be indirect, respectful, or even evasive with their employer. A woman speaking to a priest in 15th-century Spain would likely be cautious and deferential. These patterns of power and formality help shape your dialogue in ways that feel period-authentic without needing to mimic old vocabulary word for word. Ask ChatGPT, "How would a lower-class woman in 1600s London address a male doctor she doesn't trust?" or "What kind of phrases would a royal guard use when delivering bad news to a queen?"

You can also use idiomatic expressions from the era—but sparingly. One well-placed phrase can add flavor; five in a row will confuse or alienate your audience. Instead of diving into an archaic thesaurus, try selecting one or two distinctive turns of phrase for each character that hint at their time period and personality. A sailor might speak in nautical metaphors. A monk might use scripture-based speech. A merchant might sound transactional, even in personal matters. Use ChatGPT to explore these: "List common sayings used by sailors in the 18th century," or "Give me metaphors that might be used by a medieval apothecary." Pick what works and tweak it for clarity.

Tone control is also crucial. One mistake writers make is assuming that historical dialogue must always be stiff or elevated. It doesn't. People in all eras gossiped, joked, flirted, snapped at each other, and lied through their teeth. The trick is capturing those emotional beats in a way that matches the time. Sarcasm existed. So did teasing, threats, love, and embarrassment. Use ChatGPT to explore examples: "Write a sarcastic remark from a knight to his squire that feels period-appropriate," or "Give me a subtle flirtation between two nobles at a masquerade ball in 18th-century Venice." These moments humanize your characters and make the past feel alive.

One great tip is to use *modern sentence structure* with *period-informed vocabulary*. This keeps your dialogue smooth and readable while still echoing the era. Instead of writing, "Prithee, thou must take leave of mine chamber posthaste," you might write, "You've overstayed your welcome, and I'd thank you to leave now." It's still formal and sharp, but clean and accessible. Use ChatGPT to simplify dialogue when it feels clunky: "Rewrite this 18th-century letter in modern structure but with period tone," or "Polish this courtroom speech to sound old-fashioned but not overwritten."

Also, let silence do some of the talking. In historical settings—especially rigid ones—people didn't always speak their minds. Social rules could forbid direct confrontation, flirtation, or dissent. A lot of your character's intent will come through subtext. A long pause, a misdirected comment, or a sentence that trails off might carry more weight than a monologue. ChatGPT can help with this, too: "Show a passive-aggressive exchange between two courtiers vying for power," or "Write a subtle insult hidden in a toast at a Renaissance banquet." These are the moments that let history breathe in the space between words.

Don't forget emotional truth. The best dialogue sounds like what a person *would* say—not what the writer wants them to say. Ask yourself: is this how someone would express anger in this time and place? Is this what love sounded like under these conditions? If the answer feels vague, let ChatGPT help you test possibilities. "Write a declaration of love in 1930s Italy during wartime," or "How would a Puritan confess guilt without admitting sin outright?" Your job is to make the emotion feel timeless, even as the words reflect a distant past.

If you're still unsure, reverse-engineer from known works. Read a scene from *Downton Abbey*, *Peaky Blinders*, *The Last Kingdom*, or *Deadwood*—dramas that each reflect different eras and tones—and look at how their writers handled dialogue. Then try feeding similar scene ideas into ChatGPT to generate original exchanges. "Write a tense dinner scene in 1920s Berlin between a rising politician and his bohemian daughter," or "Create a dialogue between two enslaved men plotting escape in 18th-century Virginia." These results won't be perfect, but they'll give you a place to start shaping voice, pacing, and tone.

In the end, authentic historical dialogue isn't about copying old speech patterns—it's about capturing *how people sounded when they believed what they said mattered*. Keep it clear. Keep it grounded in character. Let the time period influence it without choking it. Your audience doesn't want a history lesson—they want to *feel* history unfold in the voices of people who once could have lived, breathed, and spoken like this.

Because if your characters sound alive—even in a dead language—your whole world will echo with truth.

Using ChatGPT to Craft Historical Speech Patterns

One of the fastest ways to ground your historical drama in its time and place is to give your characters a voice that reflects the world they live in. Language—specifically speech patterns—is where time travel really happens for a reader or viewer. But getting it right can be tricky. Lean too modern, and the illusion breaks. Lean too far into accuracy, and your dialogue becomes unreadable. That's where ChatGPT becomes your secret weapon. It's not just about pulling old words—it's about capturing rhythm, tone, formality, and the subtle rules that governed how people spoke, argued, begged, seduced, confessed, or betrayed each other in the past.

What makes speech *feel* historical isn't only vocabulary. It's structure. It's the cadence of thoughts. It's what people say *instead of* what they mean, and what they avoid saying altogether. And this is where ChatGPT can save you hours of mental gymnastics. Instead of trying to decode speech from old texts, you can ask the AI to generate dialogue in a specific style and then use it as a model—or as raw material to shape into your own voice.

Let's say you're writing a scene set in late 17th-century England between a merchant and a noblewoman. You could start by prompting ChatGPT with something like, "Write a short conversation between a well-mannered English merchant and a noblewoman in 1690, using appropriate speech patterns and social decorum." What you'll receive is a scene that likely includes period-appropriate formalities, indirect language, and a tone that reflects the class and gender dynamics of the time. You can then take that output and start refining—changing lines, adding subtext, or tightening the rhythm—without having to guess what an educated man of the time might have said or how a noblewoman would respond without overstepping.

Another great use of ChatGPT is to create a contrast in voices. If you're writing a story that crosses class boundaries—say, a revolutionary peasant and an aging monarch—have ChatGPT create speech for both characters and observe the differences. Try, "Write a debate between a French peasant and King Louis XVI in 1788, each using historically accurate speech patterns." You'll see right away that the king's dialogue will likely be laced with formality and detachment, while the peasant's speech might be more direct, emotional, or even poetic in its simplicity. These contrasts give your dialogue power.

If your characters are part of a specific subculture or region within a historical period, you can go even further. Ask ChatGPT, "What kind of slang would be used by sailors in 1700s England?" or "How would a 15th-century Italian nun speak to a visiting cardinal?" These more tailored queries yield better results than general time-period searches, because they pull in tone, setting, and social norms all at once.

Another trick is using ChatGPT to *translate* modern speech into period style. If you've written a scene in your own voice but want it to sound more historical, try this: paste the dialogue into ChatGPT and ask, "Rewrite this conversation to reflect 1860s American Southern speech patterns," or "Make this sound like a discussion between two Roman senators." You'll get a version that echoes the rhythms, references, and even moral tone of the time period. This technique helps you keep the emotional core of the scene while shifting the voice into historical gear.

You can also use ChatGPT to explore the *subtext* and social rules behind speech. For example, in many periods, people didn't speak openly about politics, sexuality, or betrayal. So what kind of coded language might they use instead? Ask, "How would a closeted nobleman in Victorian England discuss his feelings without saying them directly?" or "What euphemisms would be used for treason in a royal court during the Tudor era?" The answers will not only give you dialogue options—they'll teach you how to *think* like someone from that time.

Let's not forget cultural context either. Speech patterns vary wildly depending on religion, region, and education. A Puritan preacher will speak differently than a Catholic priest. A samurai will address his lord in a different manner than a Roman general would speak to his soldiers. Use ChatGPT to narrow in on these distinctions. Ask, "How would a Buddhist monk in 13th-century Japan give advice to a warrior?" or "What tone would an enslaved man in 1800s Louisiana use when speaking to his master?" These prompts help you avoid broad generalizations and instead build specificity that gives your world and characters weight.

Another way ChatGPT helps is in writing *speeches*, *letters*, or *public proclamations*. These formal moments require a different tone than everyday dialogue. They often involve elevated language, repetition, appeals to tradition or divine authority, and rhetorical questions. You can prompt the AI with, "Write a royal decree from a medieval king denouncing a traitor," or "Create a wartime letter from a Confederate soldier to his fiancée using regional dialect and period tone." Even if you end up rewriting half of it, you'll get a shape and rhythm you can't easily find just by researching online.

Finally, you can use ChatGPT to help invent your own historical dialects or speech variations for fictional cultures based on real-world models. Say you're writing a historical fantasy inspired by 14th-century Persia but set in a fictional kingdom. You can ask ChatGPT, "Blend 14th-century Persian court speech with a fictional dialect that emphasizes respect and spiritual metaphors." The AI will give you building blocks—phrases, cadences, metaphors—you can mix and match until the voice of your world starts to take shape.

The key to using ChatGPT for speech patterns is to treat it like a dialogue coach. Ask very specific questions. Feed it bits of your story and ask for rewrites. Use it to test character voice consistency. Let it offer you options, even strange ones, and don't be afraid to rewrite, reshape, and refine. You're not just using AI to mimic the past—you're collaborating with it to *sound out* a world that once was.

Because in historical drama, the words people speak are more than just dialogue. They are declarations of place, status, fear, power, and hope. They are the poetry of survival in a world we no longer live in. And when you get the speech patterns right, even your silences start to echo.

Building the Hero's Journey in the Past

The hero's journey is a timeless structure—a narrative rhythm that echoes through every genre, every culture, every era. It's the story of a person who leaves what they know, faces trials that transform them, and returns changed. In historical drama, this structure doesn't just work—it thrives. Because the past is the perfect testing ground for transformation. It's full of rules, systems, and hierarchies begging to be challenged. The stakes are often life and death, not just for the individual but for their place in society, their faith, their family name. The hero's journey isn't just a personal odyssey—it becomes a window into how people survived, rebelled, and evolved in times we only think we understand.

What makes the hero's journey in a historical setting so compelling is how *embedded* it is in the world. The journey doesn't happen outside of history—it's shaped by it, restricted by it, sometimes even caused by it. A peasant doesn't become a leader without challenging centuries of feudal law. A nun doesn't discover freedom without facing the wrath of a theocracy. Every step the hero takes rubs against the grain of their time, and that friction creates powerful storytelling.

To begin crafting the journey, you still start with the classic stages—call to adventure, refusal, mentor, trials, death/rebirth, transformation, return. But instead of inserting those into a modern framework, you wrap them in the past. Ask yourself: What was considered an adventure in this time period? What was unthinkable, un-allowed, or sacred? For some, leaving home was radical. For others, speaking out was revolutionary. Your first step is to redefine the journey's milestones through the values of the time.

Use ChatGPT to help uncover these possibilities. Ask, "What would be considered a forbidden act for a young woman in 14th-century Persia?" or "What social risks would a monk take by leaving his monastery in 12th-century France?" These moments become the cracks in tradition where your hero's journey begins.

The "call to adventure" in historical drama often comes in the form of disruption—a war, an arranged marriage, an inheritance, a secret letter, a betrayal. This moment pushes your protagonist out of their known world. But in historical drama, that "world" isn't just home. It's identity, religion, gender, caste, or reputation. Answering the call often means risking everything. You can use ChatGPT to generate story seeds: "Suggest historical inciting incidents for a hero's journey set during the fall of the Roman Empire."

The "refusal of the call" takes on extra weight in the past. Heroes didn't just hesitate because of fear—they hesitated because they understood the *weight* of tradition. In many historical societies, stepping out of line could mean exile, disgrace, or death. A samurai might refuse a journey because it violates honor. A Victorian woman might hesitate because it threatens her family's legacy. Let these fears feel real. Use ChatGPT to explore cultural consequences: "What social or religious punishments would a 17th-century Puritan woman face for rejecting her role as a wife and mother?"

Mentorship, too, takes on rich dimensions in history. A mentor could be a religious figure, a scholar, a criminal, a parent, a ghost, or a rival. They don't have to be wise in a traditional sense—just someone who sees a different path and helps the hero walk it. In historical settings, mentors are often the first whisper of another life. Ask ChatGPT, "What kind of mentor figures would exist in a medieval Islamic city for a boy interested in science?" The answers will give you not just characters—but new roads to walk.

Then come the trials—every test that pushes the hero toward growth. These should reflect the time period's reality. In modern stories, trials might involve action sequences or inner demons. In historical drama, trials are often social or existential. A woman forced to speak at a public tribunal. A soldier asked to execute an innocent man. A noble torn between duty and love. Use ChatGPT to craft them: "What kinds of moral tests could challenge a character during the Reign of Terror in France?" or "What obstacles would a runaway slave face in 1850s America?" Each trial should deepen the hero's transformation while pulling them further from the world they once knew.

The "death and rebirth" stage can be literal, but more often in historical drama, it's symbolic. A name is lost. A role is destroyed. A belief dies. Your hero is no longer who they were—and that's terrifying and liberating. This moment should be tied to the central theme of your story. If your drama is about identity, maybe your hero discards a mask. If it's about loyalty, maybe they choose truth over kin. Let this moment be stark. Let it hurt. And let it reflect the deepest contradictions of the era.

The "return with the elixir" is often bittersweet in historical settings. Your hero has changed—but the world may not welcome who they've become. A soldier returns home to find peace unbearable. A rebel re-enters the palace she once tried to burn down. A nun returns to the convent with faith transformed, no longer devout in the same way, but something new. This return often tests the *sustainability* of transformation in a world resistant to it. Ask ChatGPT, "What challenges might a woman returning home after World War I face if she's become independent and skilled?" or "How might a knight face rejection after abandoning his oath for love?"

And finally, remember that not all hero's journeys end in triumph. In historical drama, the hero may die. They may fail. But even if they lose the battle, the audience should feel that they won something more important—selfhood, clarity, peace, or truth. The hero's journey isn't just about victory. It's about meaning.

Use ChatGPT to map these arcs before you write. Try prompts like, "Plot the hero's journey for a blacksmith's daughter who becomes a revolutionary during the French Revolution," or "Create a 12-step hero's journey for a Roman slave who escapes and becomes a poet." You'll receive a skeleton to flesh out—and you can change every piece until it beats with your own rhythm.

The reason the hero's journey works so well in historical drama is because history itself is full of transformation. The world *was* changing. Empires fell. Roles dissolved. Beliefs shattered. And within those shifts, individuals either adapted—or were broken. Your hero's journey becomes a reflection of that larger movement.

Because the past isn't just where your story takes place—it's the force your hero is fighting against. And when they rise, change, or fall, they don't just tell us who they were. They show us who we are.

Emotion, Memory, and Motivation in Historical Characters

When we write historical drama, it's easy to focus on what characters did—who they fought, what laws they broke, which battles they survived or what secrets they kept. But if you stop there, you're only scratching the surface. The most powerful historical stories aren't built from action—they're built from emotion. And when emotion is woven into memory and motivation, characters stop being part of history and start *feeling* like real people who just happened to live in another time. That's where great storytelling lives—not in the past itself, but in the emotional pulse beneath it.

Historical characters are not mannequins dressed in period costumes. They are complex, frightened, proud, desperate, hopeful, angry, and loving human beings—just like we are. But they're shaped by very different forces. Their emotions are filtered through the culture, religion, family structure, and societal rules of their time. Understanding how emotion, memory, and motivation worked in their world is what gives your characters dimension. It's what makes them walk off the page.

Let's start with **emotion**. How people *feel* is always universal, but how they *express* it depends heavily on their historical context. A grieving mother in 21st-century London may openly sob in public. A grieving mother in 15th-century Japan may be expected to show silence and composure, holding pain inside to preserve her honor. Anger, shame, guilt, pride—every emotion had different acceptable expressions depending on the era and location. You can ask ChatGPT, "How was grief typically expressed by upper-class women in 18th-century France?" or "What emotional restraint was expected of soldiers in ancient Sparta?" These answers will help you avoid projecting modern behavior onto historical characters and allow you to write emotional moments that feel real to the time.

Then comes **memory**—the well your characters draw from when making decisions. Memory in historical drama works differently than it does today. Characters didn't grow up with photographs, social media, or even consistent records. Their memories were shaped by oral storytelling, family legends, religious teachings, folk traditions, and personal experience. A soldier in 1600 might remember a battle not by dates and strategy, but by the smell of blood-soaked earth, the sound of a dying horse, or a comrade's final words whispered into the mud. Memory becomes emotional, not factual—and that emotion drives character choices.

Ask ChatGPT to help build these memory layers: "What childhood memories might a girl raised in a 17th-century Dutch trading family carry into adulthood?" or "What traumatic memories would linger in a plague survivor from 14th-century Florence?" These memories don't need to be explained outright in the narrative—they can surface in gestures, hesitations, and reactions. A man who flinches at the sight of red cloth. A woman who avoids walking past the church that took her daughter. These quiet echoes make history feel lived-in and haunted in the most human way.

Now fold emotion and memory into **motivation**—because this is what makes characters act. In historical drama, characters rarely act from pure individual will. They are surrounded by rules, customs, hierarchies, religion, fear, honor, duty. Their motivations often clash with what they feel or remember, and that tension is the heartbeat of drama. A nobleman might feel compassion but be driven by legacy. A midwife might remember a past injustice but be bound by social silence. A slave might dream of escape, but stay for the sake of a hidden child.

When building motivation, ask yourself: What does the character *want*—and what are they *allowed* to want? That distinction is where history comes into play. A desire for freedom in a time of slavery isn't just a personal goal—it's a threat to the social order. A wish for knowledge in a time of censorship becomes rebellion. Use ChatGPT to probe deeper: "What motivations would drive a lower-class man to become a political agitator during the French Revolution?" or "What might motivate a nun in Renaissance Italy to break her vows?" The more pressure you put on the character's inner and outer worlds, the more layered their arc becomes.

Don't be afraid to let motivations shift over time. Just like today, people in history changed. A character who starts out motivated by pride might end up moved by guilt. Someone who seeks revenge may find peace. Those shifts—when rooted in emotion and memory—feel earned. And they reflect the instability of the world around them, which in many historical settings was changing just as quickly as they were. Wars, pandemics, revolutions, natural disasters—all of these turned ordinary lives upside down. Let your characters evolve under pressure.

Sometimes the most important motivation is *survival*. Many historical characters lived in precarious conditions—disease, war, famine, systemic violence. That struggle to survive colors every decision. A girl who lies to protect her brother. A priest who sacrifices a convert to save his parish. These aren't just dramatic moments—they're reflections of a world where living was already a victory. Ask ChatGPT, "What survival strategies might a woman use in Nazi-occupied Poland?" or "What compromises would a starving family make in Dust Bowl-era America?" These answers give you tension without needing to invent melodrama.

You can also use emotion, memory, and motivation to shape character relationships. How do two characters remember the same event differently? What emotional baggage do they carry that affects how they speak to each other? Does one person act out of love while the other acts out of guilt? These emotional mismatches create conflict without needing external enemies. They make dialogue sharp and layered. Ask ChatGPT, "Write a conversation between two brothers—one a loyalist, one a rebel—arguing about a childhood promise in Revolutionary-era Boston." You'll see how memory reshapes motivation and how emotion can deepen historical context without a single fact being stated.

And finally, use all three to shape your character's ending. When you know what your character feels, what they remember, and what drives them, their final decision—whether it's to fight, run, speak, or stay silent—will feel inevitable. It doesn't have to be heroic. It just has to be *true* to their internal landscape and the time that shaped them.

Because in historical drama, the past isn't just a backdrop. It's a pressure cooker. And emotion, memory, and motivation are what let us see how real people survived, cracked, rose, or broke under that pressure. With ChatGPT as your creative partner, you can explore all the angles—test out what someone might feel, what they might remember, what they might be desperate for—and then write them into a story that breathes.

Because when a character *feels* real, the past doesn't feel distant anymore. It feels personal. And that's the kind of historical drama that stays with your reader long after the final scene.

Fictional Characters in Real-World History

One of the most rewarding parts of writing historical drama is the freedom to blend fact with imagination. Real-world history offers the structure, the stakes, the weight—but fiction gives you the room to breathe life into characters that never existed. When you place fictional people inside actual historical events, you unlock a powerful narrative space. You get to explore the emotional truth behind the factual one. You get to ask not just what happened, but how it felt. And most importantly, you create a bridge between your audience and the past that feels personal, emotional, and human.

Fictional characters in real-world history allow you to dramatize the "what-ifs" and "what-would-you-do" moments that textbooks can't touch. You don't have to be constrained by the exact biographies of historical figures. Instead, you can place your character right on the edge of history—close enough to touch it, be changed by it, and even change it in small, invisible ways. That's where the real power of storytelling kicks in.

The first step is choosing your historical context. You want a moment or era that has weight—something that changed lives, redefined a country, challenged a system, or shook a belief. It doesn't have to be famous. In fact, sometimes the best stories come from lesser-known events: a forgotten protest, a localized tragedy, an unsung scientific discovery. The more space there is around the facts, the more room you have to invent.

Once you've chosen the setting, figure out your angle of entry. Don't try to retell the event. Let it loom in the background, moving like weather across your character's life. Ask yourself, what would it feel like to be on the sidelines of this moment? What would it cost to get involved? What if you had the chance to act but chose not to? These questions give your fictional character purpose.

Let's say you're writing about the fall of the Berlin Wall. The historical event is fixed. But you can create a character—a teenage East Berlin graffiti artist—who's watching the wall crumble, paint still drying on their final message. What does that moment mean to *them*? How did they get there? How were they shaped by the years leading up to it? Their story may be fictional, but their emotional truth is very real. It gives the reader a personal anchor in a sea of history.

You can use ChatGPT to help generate these kinds of characters. Ask, "Create a fictional character who lived through the French Revolution and was connected to the Reign of Terror in a personal way," or "Give me the profile of a working-class woman who witnessed the suffrage movement in 1900s London." These profiles give you raw material to build on—name, background, conflict, and stakes—all customized to your historical backdrop.

Fictional characters also allow you to ask risky, honest questions without rewriting real people's lives. Maybe you want to explore what it felt like to be a closeted gay man working in a government office during McCarthy-era America. Instead of using an actual historical figure, you create your own—and with him, you explore the paranoia, fear, silence, and double lives that defined the time. He might cross paths with real figures. He might attend real events. But his story is yours to tell.

When blending fiction and fact, it's important to anchor your characters in the emotional and cultural logic of the time. A fictional woman who becomes a surgeon during the Crimean War should be shaped by the constraints of Victorian society, even if she pushes against them. Her beliefs, fears, and ambitions should feel real within that world. Ask ChatGPT for help: "What obstacles would a woman face pursuing medicine in mid-19th-century Britain?" or "How might a fictional Black musician in 1920s Harlem be impacted by segregation laws while rising to fame?" These insights give your characters integrity, even if their names are made up.

You can also use fictional characters to fill the gaps history leaves behind. History rarely records the people in the background—the servants, the soldiers who didn't rise in rank, the women whose letters were burned, the children who witnessed horror and couldn't understand it. These are the people you can give a voice. A fictional character can become the conscience of an event, the witness to an atrocity, the emotional memory of something that history tried to forget.

Another trick is to use real events as the *inciting incident* or *climactic turning point* in your fictional character's arc. A political uprising can trigger a moral decision. A plague outbreak can expose deep family secrets. A royal marriage can destroy a private romance. Ask ChatGPT to help craft these moments: "Plot a fictional story of betrayal during the 1666 Great Fire of London," or "Create a love story set during the 1918 Spanish flu pandemic that ends with a political twist." The real-world event becomes the lens through which the fictional story burns brighter.

One challenge in writing fictional characters into history is avoiding historical inaccuracy while maintaining creative freedom. You don't want your character inventing antibiotics in the 1500s or tweeting from a trench in World War I. But you *can* give them ahead-of-their-time ideas, unrecorded relationships, secret knowledge, or rebellious energy—as long as it's plausible. Use ChatGPT to fact-check creative risks: "Could a woman realistically have disguised herself as a man to fight in the American Civil War?" or "Were there secret printing presses during the Inquisition?" These checks keep your fiction grounded in possibility.

Dialogue is another place where fictional characters shine. Since you're not locked into historical transcripts, you can let your characters speak with emotional honesty, even while echoing the rhythms and decorum of the era. They can ask the hard questions, say the unsayable, or give voice to what others couldn't risk speaking aloud. A fictional character can serve as a moral compass—or a tragic warning—for the world around them.

Finally, consider how your fictional character *interacts* with real figures. Maybe they serve under a famous general, work in the household of a known queen, or cross paths with a revolutionary in the marketplace. These connections add realism without requiring you to rewrite the biographies of the famous. Ask ChatGPT, "Who might a fictional servant realistically work for in Versailles during the late 1700s?" or "How could a fictional newspaper editor influence public opinion during the Dreyfus Affair?" Let these intersections become meaningful without overpowering the fictional thread.

In the end, fictional characters in real-world history allow you to write *around* the big events, not *about* them. You write through emotion, through perspective, through the details nobody thought to record. And that's where the magic happens. You make history feel like it's happening for the first time. You turn facts into feelings. You let the past breathe through people who never existed—but absolutely *could* have.

And with the right mix of research, imagination, and ChatGPT in your corner, you can tell the stories history left behind. The ones that matter not because they changed the world—but because they show what it felt like to live in the middle of it.

Inventing a World within a World

In historical drama, there's the world we know—the one found in history books, documentaries, and museum exhibits—and then there's the world your characters actually live in. The private world. The hidden world. The world inside the world. This is where your story breathes. While the broader setting gives your drama its structure—dates, geography, politics—the *invented world within that world* gives it intimacy, depth, and soul. It's what transforms your historical backdrop from a stage set into a living, personal reality shaped by your characters' inner lives, relationships, routines, and secret spaces.

Inventing this inner world means zooming in. It means choosing one alley instead of a whole city. One family instead of an entire dynasty. One street corner where secrets are whispered, or a single monastery where doubt grows in silence. It means asking not just *what happened* in history, but *what it felt like* to live through it in one particular place, at one particular moment, from one specific point of view. And ChatGPT can help you build every corner of that small, vivid world.

Let's say you're writing a historical drama set during the fall of Constantinople. That's the larger world—grand, violent, historic. But your story could be set entirely within one crumbling library guarded by a handful of terrified scribes and scholars. That library becomes your world within the world. Its inner rules, fears, routines, superstitions, alliances, and betrayals become the focus. While the empire collapses around them, your characters are just trying to save a few books, preserve a secret manuscript, or keep faith in a fading culture. That invented space gives your drama urgency and intimacy. It's where the emotional story unfolds.

You can ask ChatGPT to help you build these internal worlds. Try, "Invent a hidden apothecary shop in 16th-century Venice run by a disgraced physician," or "Describe the daily operations of a secret school for girls in 1850s Persia." The AI can help you imagine who lives there, what they do, how they survive, what rules they follow, what fears keep them quiet, and what hopes keep them alive. These settings don't have to be historically documented—they just have to feel like they could have existed in the cracks of history.

Invented worlds work especially well when your story involves marginalized voices. History often forgets the poor, the enslaved, the disabled, the outcast, the invisible. But these characters had worlds of their own. Invent a network of midwives in Elizabethan England who pass forbidden knowledge. Or a coded language used by prisoners in a 19th-century Siberian labor camp. Ask ChatGPT, "Create a believable underground resistance among orphans during the Napoleonic Wars," and watch how it sketches out a society within the margins of power.

Rituals and routines are a huge part of what make these inner worlds feel real. Maybe your characters light candles in secret every night to honor the dead. Maybe they gather once a week in a hidden courtyard to share food and forbidden books. These rituals give emotional rhythm to the story and deepen the setting. They make the place feel lived-in, shaped by time and trauma. Use ChatGPT to brainstorm: "Give me rituals for a secret society of abolitionist women in 1830s America," or "What daily routines might exist among plague doctors living in a quarantined district in 14th-century France?"

You can also invent physical spaces. Hidden rooms, underground tunnels, rooftops, gardens behind monasteries, shuttered parlours where forbidden music is played. These places don't need to appear on a historical map—they just need to feel true to the story's emotional landscape. They often reflect your characters' needs: safety, secrecy, freedom, connection. Ask ChatGPT to help visualize them: "Describe a secret courtyard in Moorish Spain used by lovers from opposing faiths," or "Invent the layout of a rebel hideout beneath a butcher's shop in 1916 Dublin."

Objects can also belong to this inner world. A single locket, a coded book, a map carved into a table, a tapestry used to signal danger. These items become emotional symbols. They tie your fictional world to the historical one while creating narrative weight. Ask ChatGPT, "What kind of objects might hold symbolic meaning to a sailor condemned to die in 18th-century Portugal?" These props make the invented world tactile and memorable.

Relationships are the emotional foundation of your invented world. Who protects whom? Who teaches the children? Who has power? Who suffers in silence? In the confined world of a Jewish ghetto during WWII, or a convent hiding runaways in 1820s Spain, relationships aren't just personal—they're strategic, dangerous, tender, coded. You can ask ChatGPT, "What kinds of roles would emerge in a hidden community of escaped slaves in the 1840s American South?" This helps you explore the social microcosms within a broader historical frame.

Even speech patterns can shift inside your invented world. The way people talk to each other privately might be entirely different from how they speak in public. A character might use a made-up language with their lover, or speak bluntly only when behind closed doors. Their voice becomes a key to intimacy and trust. Ask ChatGPT, "What kind of informal language or nicknames might be used among child factory workers in 19th-century Manchester?"

And don't forget belief systems. Your inner world can have its own codes of ethics, its own creation myths, or its own emotional truths. A group of dying soldiers might develop their own stories about the afterlife. A crew of pirates could believe in omens that guide their choices. These invented beliefs give color and shape to your characters' world. Ask ChatGPT, "Invent a spiritual belief held by gravediggers during the Black Death," or "What personal mythology might be shared among performers in a traveling 18th-century circus?"

The key to inventing a world within a world is not historical accuracy—it's emotional plausibility. Does it feel true to the time, even if it isn't recorded? Does it reflect the pressures and fears your characters live with every day? Does it give them something to hold onto when everything else is falling apart? That's the measure of success. Your readers or viewers won't care if the detail existed—they'll care that it *feels* like it could have.

And with ChatGPT by your side, you never have to invent in isolation. You can brainstorm faster, test different directions, dig deeper into cultural logic, and layer your imagined world with just enough historical flavor to make it sing. You create a past within the past—a living, breathing corner of history that no one has ever seen before.

Because sometimes, it's not the grand palace or the famous battlefield that tells the most gripping story. It's the hidden room beneath the tavern. The chapel in the forest. The eyes across the courtyard. The world within the world.

That's where the heart of your historical drama truly lives.

Writing the Big Scene That Changed Everything

Every historical drama has one. That big scene. The moment everything breaks, shifts, turns, or collapses. It's the scene your story has been building toward, the one your characters will never recover from, and the one your audience will remember long after the story ends. Sometimes it's an ambush, a betrayal, a confession, or a kiss. Sometimes it's a riot in the streets, a death in silence, a marriage gone wrong, or a secret finally spoken. This isn't just a plot twist. This is the *emotional earthquake* that changes the landscape of your story.

Writing that scene—your scene that changes everything—isn't about shock value or spectacle. It's about weight. Emotional, historical, character-based weight. It's the moment where the personal and the political collide, when the lies can't hold, when the masks come off, when someone either becomes who they truly are or loses who they used to be. And in historical drama, it's even more powerful because it's grounded in a world where change comes with consequence. When people rebel against tradition, it costs something. When people love across lines, it risks everything. When truth is spoken, it's often too late.

So how do you write it?

Start by knowing exactly what is at stake. In this scene, something important—identity, loyalty, trust, love, safety, belief—has to be on the line. It's not just about what happens but what *changes* because of it. If someone dies, it isn't powerful unless that death alters the emotional logic of the story. If a secret is revealed, it has to rupture something: a relationship, a belief, a system. Use ChatGPT to help you define the stakes. Ask, "What is the emotional cost of a servant revealing a noble's secret in a 1700s royal court?" or "What would be at risk if a soldier admitted he deserted during World War I?"

Then pinpoint whose point of view this scene belongs to. Your protagonist might be in the room—or watching from a distance. They might be the one making the choice, or they might be the one left reeling from it. What matters is that this scene hits them at their core. Their beliefs, fears, and memories should all come crashing into this moment. Let their emotional history surface—small gestures, flashes of memory, panic, fury, silence. These details make the scene feel real, not staged.

You can use ChatGPT to explore how a character might emotionally respond to a high-stakes moment. Ask, "How would a young woman raised in a convent respond emotionally to discovering her mother is a political prisoner?" or "What internal reaction might a loyal knight have to realizing his king is a traitor?"

Next, ground the scene in the sensory world. Historical dramas are most powerful when the past *feels* close. What does the room smell like? What sounds are in the distance? What is the weather doing? A rebellion that begins in the rain has a different weight than one that begins under a clear sky. Let the physical world echo the emotional shift. If a character collapses under guilt, maybe the candlelight flickers out at that exact moment. If a rebellion begins, maybe it's signalled by a distant drumbeat or the sudden silence of a city holding its breath.

Use ChatGPT to paint this world with you: "Describe the setting for a secret night-time execution in medieval Prague," or "Create the atmosphere of a royal ball where a scandal is about to unfold."

Dialogue is a crucial part of this scene, but be careful not to overwrite it. The best lines are often short, sharp, and inevitable. Let the emotion sit between the words. A single phrase—"You knew?" or "Don't lie to me"—can carry far more power than a monologue if it's been earned. Ask ChatGPT for phrasing ideas: "What might a betrayed daughter whisper to her father after discovering he sold her into marriage?" or "What would a revolutionary yell to a crowd to ignite rebellion in 19th-century Paris?"

In many cases, this scene will involve confrontation—between characters, ideologies, classes, or internal truths. Don't shy away from letting people hurt each other. Not physically, but emotionally. The best historical dramas bleed when someone says what cannot be unsaid. A wife tells her husband he's a coward in front of his soldiers. A son tells his mother he renounced her faith. A slave turns down the chance to escape to protect someone still in chains. These scenes should be hard to write. If they don't make you pause, reread, and adjust your own breathing, you haven't gone deep enough.

This scene doesn't have to be explosive. Quiet can be just as devastating. A dinner where no one speaks. A character realizing they're alone. A room left empty after everyone else flees. The change doesn't always happen through action—it often happens through *understanding*. The moment someone realizes they've lost, that they've won at too great a cost, that everything they fought for was a lie.

Pacing matters here, too. You want to slow down time without dragging it. Use shorter sentences when emotion peaks. Let the moment breathe. Let silence hang. Don't rush the revelation—revelations land harder when you let the reader sense them coming just before they hit.

And after the moment happens—after the shot is fired, the line is spoken, the kiss is rejected, the child is taken—let the world react. The consequences are everything. Who leaves? Who breaks? Who doubles down? Who loses faith? This scene changes the trajectory of the story. Ask ChatGPT, "What immediate fallout might follow a public assassination at a royal banquet in the 1500s?" or "What would happen to a noblewoman who denounces her husband in front of a church congregation in 1650s Spain?"

This is your turning point. Your break in the dam. And once it's passed, nothing in your story should be the same.

Writing the big scene that changes everything isn't about going bigger—it's about going *truer*. Truer to the character, to the time, to the emotion that's been building. You don't need explosions or armies. You just need one moment that matters. One moment that leaves a scar on your story's soul.

And when you get that moment right—when you write it with detail, weight, and emotional truth—you'll find that everything that comes before it gains new meaning. And everything that follows will be about what's left behind.

Because in historical drama, as in life, there's always that one moment we can never return from. That's the scene. And now it's yours to write.

Making Historical Events Personal

History can feel distant—written in stone, told in dates, remembered in grand speeches and epic paintings. But when you're writing historical drama, your job isn't to chronicle what happened. Your job is to *humanize* it. To make it personal. Because the truth is, every historical event—no matter how famous or forgotten—was once someone's *worst day*, someone's *private heartbreak*, someone's *moment of decision*. It wasn't just war, revolution, or change. It was the day someone didn't come home, the night someone couldn't sleep, the moment someone lied, confessed, broke, or tried to be brave.

Making historical events personal means getting under the skin of history. It means asking not just, "What happened?" but "How did it feel to live through it?" It means finding the emotional thread that connects a reader or viewer to a character standing on the edge of something far bigger than themselves. And once you find that thread, you pull it tight and never let go.

Let's say your story takes place during the Great Depression. That's your event—your context. But instead of writing a sweeping story about banks collapsing and the dust bowl rolling in, you zoom in on one family. Maybe it's a teenage girl watching her father quietly pawn his wedding ring. Or a mother trying to make a soup stretch for three days without showing fear in her eyes. That's how you make the big picture personal—by showing how it changes the little moments, the relationships, the silences. You're writing not about the Depression itself, but what it does *to people*.

You can use ChatGPT to help you dig deeper into these angles. Ask, "What everyday struggles would a single father face during the 1930s in rural Kansas?" or "How might a child secretly observe the impact of the Great Depression on their parents' marriage?" The more specific you get, the more emotional material you have to work with.

Sometimes, the most powerful way to personalize history is through a character who doesn't understand the full weight of what's happening. A young boy watching soldiers march through his village. A servant overhearing news of a king's execution. A woman waiting at a train station for someone who isn't coming back. These are moments where the audience *knows* the history—but the character only feels it. That emotional disconnect creates tension, irony, and heartbreak all at once.

You can also bring history closer by focusing on *small decisions with big consequences*. A letter not sent. A bribe accepted. A secret shared in confidence. In a historical setting, even the quietest choices can echo loudly. Ask ChatGPT, "What would be the risk of refusing to spy for the Stasi in 1970s East Germany?" or "How might a housemaid quietly sabotage a family's support of the Nazi party?" These kinds of personal actions, when set against the backdrop of history, give your characters agency and moral complexity.

Another technique is using **relationships** to filter history. We often think of events in terms of winners and losers, heroes and villains—but drama happens in the spaces in between. A loyalist father and a revolutionary son during the American Revolution. A Catholic mother and a Protestant daughter in Northern Ireland during the Troubles. A Japanese soldier and a Chinese civilian caught in an impossible moment during wartime. These relationships give history a beating heart. They allow you to dramatize opposing views without losing the personal stakes.

If you're stuck, try asking ChatGPT for relationship-driven setups: "Create a fictional story about two lovers on opposite sides of the Spanish Civil War," or "What conflicts might arise between two sisters in 18th-century Paris as the Revolution begins?" These setups give you fertile ground to explore how history drives people apart—or brings them together.

Personalizing history also means using **internal conflict**. Your character might believe in something that history is tearing apart. A priest who starts doubting God during the Black Death. A patriot who becomes disillusioned with the revolution he helped start. A doctor who can't save lives during a cholera outbreak and starts drinking in secret. These emotional fractures tell us more about history than any list of laws or battles ever could.

Even physical spaces can personalize history. A family home slowly falling apart as war looms. A shop once bustling with customers now quiet with fear. A schoolroom turned into a field hospital. Let your characters move through spaces that reflect what's happening outside. Ask ChatGPT to help: "Describe a house during World War II as the family inside prepares for evacuation," or "What changes would a Jewish-owned bookstore in Berlin undergo in the late 1930s?" These sensory shifts turn history into something lived, not studied.

And remember—your characters don't need to be leaders or heroes. They can be ordinary people swept into extraordinary times. A baker. A tailor. A child. A nurse. A gravedigger. A seamstress sewing coded messages into dresses. These are the voices that history rarely writes down, but fiction can illuminate. You can ask ChatGPT to create characters like this: "Invent a working-class man who witnesses the fall of the Bastille," or "Create a young girl hiding in a barn during the Warsaw Uprising." These are your windows into the past.

Finally, consider your audience. Why should someone today care about something that happened hundreds of years ago? The answer is always emotional truth. We still grieve. We still fear. We still hope. The technologies have changed. The costumes have changed. But the hearts beating inside the story? They're the same. So when you make history personal, you remind the reader that it isn't just about then—it's about *now*. It's about us.

So go beyond the timelines. Step inside the kitchens, the bedrooms, the fields, the churches, the prison cells. Listen to what the characters are afraid to say. What they hope for in the dark. What they whisper to their children before sleep. And let those moments guide the story.

Because once history becomes personal, it becomes unforgettable.

Love, War, Revolution: Big Themes in Historical Drama

Some themes never go out of style. They show up in every generation, in every era, across every culture. Love. War. Revolution. These are the big ones—the elemental forces that rip through personal lives and shake entire societies. In historical drama, these themes aren't just backdrop—they're fire. They give shape to the character arcs, the emotional turns, and the moral crossroads that drive the story forward. But to make them work in historical storytelling, you have to do more than just drop them into a costume drama. You have to root them in the emotional and cultural soil of the time. When you do that, love becomes more than romance, war becomes more than battle, and revolution becomes more than slogans.

Let's start with **love**. In a modern story, love is usually a matter of choice. In historical drama, it's often a matter of *defiance*. Love means breaking rules—class barriers, religious restrictions, family expectations, even national loyalty. That's why historical love stories carry so much weight. Every stolen glance or whispered promise carries the risk of exile, shame, or death. The stakes are never just emotional—they're systemic. A knight falling for a commoner, a queen secretly writing letters to a poet, a soldier in love with someone on the other side of the war—these stories work because love threatens the entire structure of the world around them.

To make love feel real in historical drama, focus on what it costs. What does your character have to give up, hide, or fight for to be with the one they love? Ask ChatGPT for help digging into this: "What social consequences would a noblewoman face for loving a merchant in 17th-century Spain?" or "How could two women have secretly maintained a relationship in Victorian London?" These situations become more than emotional—they become dramatic engines for your story.

Now shift to **war**. War in historical drama isn't just explosions and strategy. It's disruption. It's grief. It's transformation. It's the force that pushes people out of their comfort zones and into survival mode. But it's also a mirror—it reveals who your characters really are when the world falls apart. And it affects everyone differently. Soldiers on the front lines. Wives left behind. Children hiding under the floorboards. Priests trying to comfort the dying. Shopkeepers trying to survive with no supplies. Every perspective gives you a new angle on war as theme—not just war as setting.

When writing about war, you don't always need battlefield scenes. Some of the most powerful war stories are told through the aftermath—the long silence after a bombing, the empty chair at the dinner table, the smell of gunpowder that never leaves someone's coat. Use ChatGPT to explore this quieter side: "Describe the emotional impact on a farmer returning to his land after the Civil War," or "What daily struggles would a woman face trying to keep a household running during World War I?" These moments give the war meaning far beyond maps and medals.

And then there's **revolution**. Revolution is about more than just politics—it's about identity, rage, hope, and consequence. In historical drama, a revolution can be grand—marches, manifestos, executions—or deeply personal: a servant refusing to bow, a scholar publishing forbidden ideas, a mother teaching her daughter to read in secret. Revolution is the heartbeat of historical drama because it captures the tension between what is and what could be. Between power and resistance. Between tradition and change.

But to write it well, you have to understand the *why*. Why are people rising up? What's broken in their world? What are they willing to risk to change it? A revolution isn't just an event—it's a test of character. Not everyone fights on the same side. Not everyone agrees on what justice looks like. Ask ChatGPT, "What internal divisions existed among revolutionaries during the Russian Revolution?" or "How might a young man be torn between loyalty to the crown and belief in the American cause?" These questions help you build complexity into your revolution. Because the best ones aren't black and white. They're messy, emotional, and deeply human.

What ties these three themes—love, war, and revolution—together is that they all challenge the *status quo*. They force characters to choose. To reveal themselves. To grow—or break. And in historical drama, the stakes are higher because the systems are often more rigid. There's less room for error, less room to run. Every act of love, violence, or rebellion shakes the world just a little more.

That's why blending these themes often leads to the most gripping stories. A love affair that sparks a revolution. A soldier who deserts for love. A child who loses their parents to war and grows into a revolutionary leader. These arcs don't have to be complicated—they just have to be emotionally true. Ask ChatGPT to help you merge themes: "Create a character arc for a young woman who falls in love with a rebel during a revolution," or "Build a story outline where a soldier's act of kindness changes the course of a war."

You don't have to write a sweeping epic. Sometimes, the biggest themes live in the smallest spaces—a letter passed between lovers at the edge of a battlefield. A revolution whispered in a church basement. A child hiding under the bed while their world burns down. The trick is to let the big themes live through personal choices. Through quiet defiance. Through moments of tenderness in a brutal world.

Because when you write love, war, and revolution in a historical setting, you're not just telling a story about what people did. You're telling a story about what they *felt* while they did it. The fear. The longing. The guilt. The courage. The hope that something could still matter, even when the world was falling apart.

So lean into the scale. Embrace the mess. And let your characters feel everything. Because history remembers the facts—but drama remembers the feeling. And that's where your story lives.

Building Tragedy from the Truth

Historical drama lends itself so naturally to tragedy because, at its core, it's grounded in real human limitation. You're working with characters who are bound by time, culture, law, status, faith, or fate—and you already know that many of them won't make it out unscathed. The truth is, history itself is a graveyard of what could have been. It's full of broken dreams, silenced voices, betrayals, wars, and revolutions that ended in blood. When you build tragedy from truth, you're not just telling a sad story. You're writing something deeply resonant—a drama that lingers, because it was always heading this way. It was in the bones of the story all along.

But good tragedy isn't about hopelessness. It's about inevitability. It's about watching someone walk a path you know they can't come back from. It's about watching a flaw play out against pressure that won't bend. In historical drama, that pressure is often built into the setting itself. A woman born into a patriarchal society can try to rise, but her defiance will cost her. A child raised inside a cult of loyalty may try to rebel—but can't betray their father. A soldier who has seen too much will try to return home—but the home no longer exists.

This is the emotional power of history: your characters are trying to be free in a world that won't allow it. And the tragedy comes not from how they fail—but *why* they fail.

So how do you build that?

Start by grounding the tragedy in the historical reality. What systems were in place that your character can't escape? What laws, traditions, or social expectations trap them? Use ChatGPT to help identify these historical constraints. Ask, "What societal pressures would a young woman face if she refused marriage in 16th-century China?" or "What punishments existed for political dissent in Stalinist Russia?" These facts aren't just backdrop—they're the forces tightening around your character's story.

Then, focus on the emotional contradiction. The most powerful tragic characters are those who *want something deeply*, and that desire collides with the very thing they cannot control. A samurai who values honor above all else—but must choose between loyalty and truth. A priest who believes in mercy—but must carry out a brutal law. A mother who would do anything to protect her child—but is forced to give them up to survive. Tragedy is born in these fractures. In the moments where there is no right answer. Just loss, pain, and difficult choices.

Let ChatGPT help you explore these contradictions: "Create a character torn between love and loyalty during the French Revolution," or "What internal conflict might plague a doctor forced to choose who lives during a cholera outbreak in 1800s London?" These character dilemmas shape your tragic arc.

Structure plays a key role in tragedy. The audience should feel the outcome coming—not in a predictable way, but in a slow-building dread. The moment the character makes a small, understandable decision that sets them on a path they can't turn back from—that's where the tragedy starts. The rest of the story just peels back what that choice cost. Think of it like watching a ship drift toward rocks you know are there, but the captain doesn't. That ache, that helplessness, is what makes tragedy so devastating.

Use ChatGPT to outline this build: "Plot a tragic arc for a nobleman who becomes corrupted by power during the Roman Republic's collapse," or "Map the downfall of a freedom fighter who compromises too much in a post-colonial regime." The key is that the character must play a role in their own downfall. They can be victims of history, yes—but their choices, flaws, or blind spots help history finish the job.

And don't forget the relationships. Tragedy always hits harder when it impacts others. When love is lost, trust is shattered, families are torn apart, or a community turns on one of its own. A single betrayal can break a heart. A quiet farewell can haunt a generation. Think of how those around your main character change or suffer as the tragedy unfolds. Ask ChatGPT, "What ripple effects might a failed political assassination have on a family in 1930s Italy?" or "How might a village react to one of their own being executed for heresy in medieval Spain?" The tragedy becomes more than personal—it becomes generational.

Another important layer in historical tragedy is silence. Not everything needs to be said. In many historical settings, characters were not allowed to speak their truth. So show what they can't say. Let grief sit in the space between words. Let love die without being confessed. Let a decision go unspoken because the risk of saying it aloud is too great. ChatGPT can help you with subtle dialogue or subtext-heavy scenes: "Write a farewell between two lovers who cannot acknowledge their relationship during the Inquisition." These moments deepen the pain because they reveal everything that had to remain hidden.

You can also build tragedy from *hope*. Some of the most gut-wrenching historical dramas are the ones where the character believes, right until the end, that they'll win. That love will overcome. That justice will be served. That their sacrifice means something. Let them hope. Let the audience hope with them. And then, when the truth lands, let it break everything.

Ask ChatGPT to explore endings that reflect this emotional curve: "What tragic yet meaningful ending might suit a runaway slave who helps others escape during the Civil War?" or "Give a bittersweet conclusion for a character who exposes corruption in the 1930s but loses everything." These kinds of endings leave scars—and that's exactly what you want.

Lastly, remember that tragedy doesn't mean despair. It means *impact*. The goal isn't to crush the reader—it's to *move* them. A tragedy that feels earned leaves behind wisdom, beauty, and a sense of inevitability that can't be shaken. Your character may not survive, but their story will.

Because when tragedy grows from truth—when it's shaped by the era, born from the character, and delivered with emotional honesty—it lingers. It teaches. It haunts. And that's what historical drama, at its best, is meant to do.

How to Start Writing Without Knowing All the History

One of the biggest myths in writing historical drama is that you have to know *everything* before you begin. That unless you've studied the era like a scholar, memorized the fashion, the politics, the food, the tools, and the etiquette, you have no business starting the story. But here's the truth: you don't need to be a historian to write historical drama. You need to be a *storyteller*. Someone who knows how to feel their way through a moment. Someone who can ask the right questions, follow emotional truth, and build a world that's convincing—not because it's perfectly accurate—but because it feels lived in.

So if you've got an idea that takes place in the past, but you're overwhelmed by all the gaps in your historical knowledge, don't let that stop you. Start writing. Start exploring. Start *playing*. You can fill in the facts as you go. That's the beauty of storytelling in the age of AI—you've got a research assistant in your pocket, and ChatGPT never sleeps.

The first thing to understand is that the emotional core of your story doesn't need history to exist. Love, betrayal, ambition, fear, survival—these things are timeless. Whether your character is a 14th-century midwife or a World War II pilot, they're still trying to protect something, reach for something, or escape something. Start there. Write a scene. Any scene. Don't worry yet if the medicine is accurate or if they're wearing the right shoes. Focus on the moment: who they are, what they want, what's in their way.

Then, as those scenes begin to take shape, you can start layering in the historical details. And that's where ChatGPT comes in. You don't need to stop writing for days to do deep research. You can ask questions as you go. "What kind of food would a working-class family eat in 1910s Berlin?" "What weapons would a samurai carry in 1500s Japan?" "What kind of punishments existed for thieves in medieval France?" You don't need to know everything—you just need to know what your *scene* needs.

Let the story guide the research, not the other way around.

Sometimes, the trick is starting with a vibe rather than a date. You might say, "I want to write about a woman hiding in a crumbling city while her government collapses." You don't have to pick the exact place and time right away. You can ask ChatGPT to help you brainstorm settings that match the emotional tone: "Give me historical moments where cities were falling and ordinary people were trying to survive." You'll get possibilities—Berlin in 1945, Baghdad in 1258, Constantinople in 1453—and you can choose the one that feels right for your character.

And don't be afraid to *invent* while you're still unsure. If you're writing a story set in ancient Mesopotamia, but you don't know how a house would be laid out or what clothes people wore, just make it up for now. Use placeholders. Keep moving. Later, you can go back and adjust the details once you've done the research. The key is not letting the unknown stop your momentum.

There's a wonderful freedom in admitting you don't know everything. It keeps you curious. It keeps your writing alive. And it allows you to collaborate with history rather than feel crushed by it. Every time you hit a question—big or small—you can toss it to ChatGPT: "What did people use to light their homes in 18th-century rural England?" or "Would a Roman soldier have understood the concept of PTSD?" The answers might surprise you, deepen your story, and open new doors.

You can also work backward. Maybe you've written a scene where a woman runs barefoot through the streets after curfew. Now you ask: "What cities had curfews enforced in the 1700s, and what would happen if someone broke them?" Suddenly, you've got a location, a political tension, and a new piece of worldbuilding—all because you followed a gut-level scene and trusted you could build the history around it.

Another approach is writing in *emotional sketches*. Create a scene between a mother and daughter, or two friends, or a prisoner and their guard. Don't worry yet if the titles, ranks, or historical references are right. Just feel out the dynamic. Then go back later and ask, "What kind of relationship would be possible between a noblewoman and her servant in 1600s Spain?" ChatGPT will help shape the container, but *you* fill it with the human truth.

Sometimes the pressure to "get it right" keeps writers from starting at all. But the reality is, even historians debate what's true. New research changes old assumptions. What matters in historical drama isn't flawless accuracy—it's authenticity. A sense that the characters feel real, the world has texture, and the emotional stakes are clear. And that doesn't require memorizing a timeline. It requires empathy, imagination, and curiosity.

You don't even need to start with characters. You can begin with an image. A crumbling church in the middle of a forest. A letter burned in a fireplace. A man waiting for a verdict in a courtroom lit by candles. Ask ChatGPT, "Give me five possible historical moments when this scene could take place," and let the story form around the image. This keeps the process playful, intuitive, and grounded in your own creative instincts.

Remember, you can always go back and polish. You can revise the clothes, the setting, the technology, the laws. What you can't fake is emotional truth. That's why starting before you know everything is not just okay—it's often better. It keeps you focused on what matters. The characters. The stakes. The decisions.

So don't wait. Don't let history intimidate you. Write the scene. Ask the question. Then write the next scene. You're not building a textbook—you're building a living, breathing story. One heartbeat at a time. And every time you say, "I don't know this yet," you're not failing. You're just creating the space where discovery happens.

That's how real historical drama is born—not from certainty, but from *curiosity*. From being willing to write first, and research just enough to keep the story moving forward. The past is waiting. You don't need permission. You just need a blank page—and the courage to begin.

Writing Through the Eyes of the Forgotten

History tends to remember the loudest voices—the kings, the generals, the revolutionaries, the conquerors. But for every name etched into a monument, there are a thousand more who lived and died quietly, their stories buried under the weight of official records. Writing historical drama through the eyes of the forgotten is about lifting the veil on those lives. It's about giving voice to the voiceless. It's about telling the truth behind the curtain, where the cooks, slaves, servants, stable boys, field hands, laundresses, orphans, and prisoners watched empires rise and fall from the shadows.

And this is where the most powerful, soul-stirring stories often lie.

When you write from the margins of history, you're not limited—you're free. Because there's often less documentation, fewer rules, and more creative space. You get to fill in the silences with emotional truth. You get to imagine what it was like to live a life no one thought worthy of record. And when you do it with care, curiosity, and empathy, you give your readers something they didn't expect: a new perspective on a world they thought they already knew.

It starts with asking a very simple question: who's not in the history books?

That question cracks everything open. It might lead you to a scullery maid in a Roman villa. A deaf boy in a Revolutionary War camp. A grieving widow in an Ottoman village. A servant in a plantation kitchen. A monk who doubted the teachings he was forced to copy. These people were there. They watched. They lived history without having the power to shape it—or so it seemed.

Use ChatGPT to help you explore their world. Ask, "What was daily life like for a teenage girl working in a Victorian textile mill?" or "What would a kitchen slave have seen during a royal banquet in 18th-century Haiti?" The answers you get may be fragments—but those fragments can become emotional anchors for full scenes.

When you write from the eyes of the forgotten, *perspective* becomes your most valuable tool. These characters don't have access to power, but they often see it more clearly than those who wield it. They overhear secrets, feel the weight of decisions made by others, and suffer the consequences without recognition. This makes them rich with insight—and perfect for dramatic tension. A maid might know who the real killer is. A gravedigger might overhear a plot that could change the kingdom. A midwife might carry knowledge that would shake a patriarchal society to its knees.

But you don't need to make them heroes or spies. Let them be *people*. Let their small lives carry big meaning. Let their fears be private and real. Let their joys be rare but hard-earned. Let their losses be quiet and devastating. You can ask ChatGPT for emotional context: "What would a laundress in 1920s New York City worry about most on a normal day?" or "Describe how a child would interpret war if they lived in the ruins of post-WWI France."

Language is important, too. These characters probably wouldn't speak in grand, eloquent speeches. Their voices might be quiet, cautious, earthy, raw, or poetic in a very grounded way. Use ChatGPT to develop their dialogue: "Write a short scene between two factory workers on a break in 1890s Chicago," or "Create an interior monologue for a washerwoman watching a parade of nobles pass by." These voices carry the real emotional weight of an era. They make history feel lived-in rather than observed.

Another powerful technique is to use proximity to power without access to it. Maybe your character serves in the background of a major historical event—a messenger at Versailles, a stable boy during the Battle of Waterloo, a nurse watching a dictator die. They are close enough to feel the heat of history, but not close enough to shape it directly. That tension is gold. Ask ChatGPT, "How might a stable hand experience the day Napoleon escaped from Elba?" or "What would a street performer see during the storming of the Bastille?" These aren't just fresh angles—they're emotional entry points.

Memory also plays a huge role. Forgotten characters often live in a space of remembering what was taken, what was never theirs, or what they quietly endured. Their memories—especially if they're older—become a narrative tool. A woman telling her granddaughter about the day the soldiers came. A man whispering a name he never got to say aloud. These moments let you layer history with ache and truth. They let the personal stand beside the monumental.

If you're writing in first person, that intimacy can be even more powerful. A child who doesn't understand the significance of the event unfolding around them can tell a heartbreaking story without ever needing historical context. A servant who has no say in the decisions that shape their life can still tell you everything about the people who do. Use ChatGPT to help draft these internal voices: "Write a first-person reflection from a child hiding in a church during a massacre," or "Create a diary entry from a young woman tending the wounded after a battle she doesn't fully understand."

The beauty of writing through the eyes of the forgotten is that you don't have to explain history. You *live* in it. You see how it affects someone who can't escape it. And in doing so, you invite your audience to step out of the grand narrative and into the truth behind the truth.

Because every event we study—the wars, the laws, the revolutions—happened to someone we'll never know. But through fiction, we can give them a voice. A name. A moment of clarity. A piece of the light.

You don't need to make them famous. You just need to make them *matter*.

Because when the forgotten are remembered, even in fiction, something in history starts to feel more whole. And your story—quiet, brave, and human—becomes a kind of justice.

Letting Conflict Shape Plot and Character Together

In historical drama, conflict isn't just a plot device—it's the crucible where both story and character are forged. It's not enough to place your characters in the middle of a war, a revolution, a scandal, or a family feud. That's setting the stage. The real work comes in letting that conflict *do something* to them. Push them. Break them. Reveal them. The best historical drama doesn't just use conflict to move the story forward—it lets conflict *shape* the characters as it shapes the plot, turning the past into personal transformation.

Conflict in this context is never one-dimensional. It's not just character vs. character. It's character vs. society, character vs. tradition, character vs. expectation, and often, character vs. self. And when you do it right, the story's external tensions and the character's internal dilemmas reflect one another in perfect harmony—each one feeding, twisting, and deepening the other.

Let's say your story is about a young soldier in the American Civil War. The obvious external conflict is survival—battle, orders, hunger, death. But what if the character's internal conflict is that he no longer believes in the cause? Now, every skirmish becomes a personal reckoning. Every order followed is a betrayal of self. And every moment of inaction is loaded with fear, guilt, and identity crisis. That's how conflict doesn't just move the plot—it *builds* the character.

Use ChatGPT to help weave this together. Ask, "What internal conflicts might a Civil War soldier face after discovering his unit is responsible for war crimes?" or "How could a young woman in Tudor England struggle with loyalty to a queen she loves but knows is committing atrocities?" These tensions aren't just emotional—they're story-generating engines. They guide choices. And choices are where plot and character meet.

Another way to let conflict shape both plot and character is by focusing on the *personal stakes* of a larger historical struggle. Don't just write about the fall of a city—write about a teacher who's trying to save one last student before the gates are breached. Don't just write about a peasant uprising—write about a brother who's on one side and a sister on the other. When your characters are *of* the time period and *inside* the historical conflict, the story feels inevitable, not artificial.

And not every conflict has to be violent or loud. In many historical contexts, just wanting something forbidden can create explosive tension. A woman wanting to own land. A monk questioning scripture. A child questioning a parent's belief. These are quiet conflicts, but they carry enormous weight because the cost of stepping out of line is often total: social ruin, imprisonment, death. Ask ChatGPT for help creating this friction: "What would happen if a 19th-century Russian noble publicly criticized the Tsar?" or "How might a young Catholic girl in 1500s England hide her Protestant faith from her family?" These setups don't just create conflict—they define who your character becomes in response.

That's the real function of conflict in historical drama: *transformation*. Your character begins in one place—naive, complicit, hopeful, cowardly—and ends somewhere else because conflict didn't allow them to stay the same. They had to adapt, retreat, confront, or collapse. And with each turn of the plot, the conflict should narrow their options and force decisions that cost them something real.

Let's say you're writing a story set during the French Revolution. Your character begins as a loyal servant in a noble household. As conflict builds—bread riots, executions, betrayals—he's pulled between loyalty and survival. Maybe he hides his noble employers. Maybe he betrays them. Either way, the *choice* comes from conflict. And the choice pushes the plot forward while defining the kind of person he becomes. Ask ChatGPT to brainstorm that tension: "Outline the conflicting pressures faced by a servant in Versailles during the early stages of the Revolution."

Another powerful technique is *mirroring*. Let the external conflict echo the character's internal conflict. If a country is divided, let your character be divided. If the government is collapsing, maybe the family is, too. If a new world is being born, maybe your character is trying to become someone new. These mirrors let your theme carry through the story without ever needing to state it outright. Ask ChatGPT, "Create a storyline where a nation's political collapse parallels a character's psychological breakdown." These mirrored arcs create layered, emotionally rich storytelling.

Conflict also deepens relationships. Lovers separated by ideology. Friends torn apart by class. Mentors disappointed by their students. These are the emotional hooks that keep your audience invested. And they all come from conflict that hits close to home. Use ChatGPT to test these dynamics: "Write a scene between two brothers on opposite sides of the Civil War debating over dinner," or "Give me a confrontation between a noblewoman and her maid after the maid joins a rebellion."

And then there's the aftermath. Conflict doesn't just shape who the character becomes—it leaves a mark. Regret. Guilt. Freedom. Power. That's the final layer—letting conflict carry consequences. Maybe the character got what they wanted but lost who they were. Maybe they survived, but at the cost of someone else. Let those consequences settle into the character's soul, and let them ripple into every scene that follows.

If you ever feel stuck, ask ChatGPT to create plot-character conflict intersections. Try, "Create a turning point where a character's belief is challenged by a real-world event," or "What historical event could force a pacifist to commit violence?" These moments become emotional catalysts that drive the rest of the story.

In the end, the best historical dramas aren't just about what happened. They're about *who* it happened to—and what they did when it did. Conflict is the bridge between plot and character. It's the hammer that shapes the soul of your story. Let it strike hard, and let the sparks light up every decision, every betrayal, every silence, every stand.

Because when plot and character evolve together through conflict, your story doesn't just tell history—it *feels* like history. Lived. Unfolding. And unforgettable.

Pacing Your Historical Drama for Maximum Impact

Pacing is the rhythm your story walks to—and in historical drama, it's everything. Get the pace wrong, and your beautiful, well-researched scenes might feel like a history lecture or a rushed tour through a museum. But get the pace right, and your story breathes. It builds tension, holds emotion, and keeps the reader or viewer glued to the moment, feeling every beat of heartbreak, resistance, or revelation as if it were happening right now.

The trick with historical drama is that it's often built on two tracks at once: the *internal* emotional journey of the characters, and the *external* pressure of historical events unfolding around them. Your pacing has to serve both. And the secret isn't in speeding up or slowing down—it's in knowing *when* to do either. You want to stretch time when something emotional or dangerous is unfolding. You want to move quickly when the story needs momentum. And you want to know when to stop altogether—those rare, beautiful pauses that say everything without saying anything at all.

A great way to think about pacing is like music. Every scene has a tempo. A charged courtroom debate might be a snare drum roll—tight and rising. A quiet moment between lovers in a candlelit room might be a slow, haunting cello. Your job as the writer is to arrange the notes in a way that tells the story but also makes us *feel* the rhythm of history moving forward, sometimes too fast, sometimes too slow, sometimes just right.

Start by deciding what kind of story you're telling. If your historical drama is centered on a single event—say, the week leading up to an execution, or the final days of a war—you'll want a tighter pace. Short chapters or scenes. Ticking clocks. Constant tension. But if your story spans years—such as the life of a revolutionary or the collapse of an empire—you can allow for more breathing room. Let moments simmer. Let characters reflect. Just don't lose momentum. Even in slow scenes, something *internal* must be changing.

You can use ChatGPT to help map this out. Try, "Outline a historical drama structure that builds tension over a 24-hour period," or "Break down a multi-decade historical story into key turning points to manage pacing." These kinds of frameworks help you see the architecture of your story before you start layering in detail.

One of the most powerful pacing tools in historical drama is the contrast between *quiet and chaos*. Don't just keep ramping things up—let them fall silent at the right moment. After a brutal battle, maybe your character washes blood from their hands in silence. After a political betrayal, maybe we just sit in the quiet room where a letter has been opened. Those pauses aren't slow—they're heavy. They're moments where the audience leans in, not out.

Use ChatGPT to craft these moments: "Write a quiet, emotionally loaded scene between two characters after a public execution in 17th-century England." You'll see how less action can mean more impact.

Dialogue and sentence rhythm also shape pacing. Long, flowing monologues slow things down. Short, clipped exchanges speed it up. Think of a royal banquet—lavish, formal, slow-paced—versus a nighttime chase through war-torn streets. Let the pace match the energy of the scene. And let characters speak differently depending on the moment. In a scene where a general plans a siege, you might want tension, speed, strategy. But when he confesses fear to his lover? Slow it down. Let the cracks show.

Historical exposition is where pacing often suffers. We've all read or seen those moments where a story grinds to a halt so someone can explain a law, a battle, a royal family tree. Don't do that. Instead, weave exposition into action or dialogue. Let characters *need* the information in order to act. Let them *argue* over the meaning of an event. Let them *misunderstand* history in a way that reveals who they are. Ask ChatGPT, "How can I explain the Edict of Nantes in a dramatic scene between a Protestant and a Catholic during a riot in 1598?" Now the history serves the story—not the other way around.

You can also use pacing to reflect historical pressure. If your story is set during a plague, let the scenes become more disjointed and desperate as the illness spreads. If it's during an uprising, let the tempo build toward chaos. If your characters are waiting—on a letter, a verdict, a war to end—slow the pacing to reflect that agonizing stillness. The structure of your story should mimic the tension of the time.

Flashbacks and time jumps are another way to control pacing in historical drama. They allow you to condense years into pages, or open up emotional backstory in the middle of high-stakes action. Just use them with purpose. Flashbacks should reveal character or deepen stakes—not just show cool historical moments. ChatGPT can help you structure this: "Create a story outline that uses alternating timelines to reveal a family secret during the Russian Revolution." This helps you pace revelations, which keeps the audience engaged.

And then there's the climax. The payoff. The big moment you've been building toward. Here, your pacing should tighten like a noose. Shorter scenes. Sharper decisions. Less wandering. More urgency. Everything should be converging. Use pacing to pull every thread taut—emotionally and structurally. Ask ChatGPT, "Design a rising tension sequence leading to the execution of a falsely accused noble in Renaissance Florence." You'll see how pacing acts like gravity—pulling everything toward the final moment.

But don't let the ending rush. After the climax, give your characters space to absorb what's changed. That's where the emotional weight lands. Maybe it's a quiet departure. A letter written in silence. A final look at a ruined home. This moment of reflection gives the story closure and lets the reader feel the cost of what's happened.

In the end, pacing is about balance. Motion and stillness. Noise and quiet. Detail and restraint. And historical drama gives you the perfect canvas to use all of it. You've got the backdrop of real events and the heartbeat of human truth. Let one drive the plot and the other shape the tempo. And if you're ever unsure, trust the rhythm of the emotion. Let the scene breathe when it hurts. Let it rush when it thrills. Let it linger when something needs to sink in.

Because when you pace your story with emotional precision, every moment feels necessary. Every pause feels earned. And every beat feels alive.

Getting Unstuck with ChatGPT Midway through the Story

Every writer hits the wall. That moment halfway through your historical drama when the scenes don't land, the characters won't speak, and the plot feels like it's stuck in mud. Maybe you've lost the thread of your main arc. Maybe your story doesn't feel exciting anymore. Maybe you wrote yourself into a corner with a historical detail and now can't see a way forward. Whatever the reason, it happens. It's part of the process. And the good news is, you don't have to claw your way out alone.

This is where ChatGPT becomes more than a writing tool—it becomes a creative partner. A sounding board. A pressure release valve. And sometimes, a spark that gets the whole thing moving again. The trick isn't just throwing your whole story at the AI and asking it to fix it. It's knowing *how* to ask for help—how to break your problem into parts and invite in a fresh perspective.

Let's say you're halfway through a story set during the Irish War of Independence. You've got your characters, your stakes, and your world—but now the momentum's gone. The story feels flat. One way to get unstuck is to start asking questions that aren't about the plot itself but about the *characters inside the plot*. You can ask ChatGPT, "What are three secrets this character might be hiding that could add tension?" or "What past event might come back to haunt my protagonist at this point in the story?" These answers often lead to new scenes, twists, and revelations that re-energize the entire middle of your script or novel.

Another way to break through is to shift perspective. Midway through a historical drama is the perfect time to look at the events from a different lens. Maybe the antagonist gets a chapter. Maybe a side character has a revelation. Maybe you tell a flashback that changes the meaning of everything that's happened so far. Ask ChatGPT, "Write a scene from the perspective of a secondary character watching the protagonist make a critical mistake," or "What event from five years earlier could suddenly become relevant now?"

Sometimes what you really need is to re-map the structure. That doesn't mean starting over. It means stepping back and checking your compass. You can say to ChatGPT, "Here's what's happened so far..." and give a short summary of your chapters or scenes. Then ask, "Based on this, what are three directions the story could go next that raise the stakes?" or "What internal conflict could surface now that would tie into the story's theme?" The AI can help identify patterns you may not have noticed or suggest thematic threads to pull on.

Midway is also when you start feeling the weight of research. Maybe you've hit a historical snag—something doesn't line up. Maybe a real-world event throws a wrench into your fictional plot. Instead of freezing, let ChatGPT help you pivot. Ask, "What plausible workaround could I use if I want a character to travel between Paris and Berlin during wartime in 1942?" or "What historical event could cause a sudden separation between two lovers in 1840s China?" You're not giving up on accuracy—you're using flexibility to stay focused on the story's emotional engine.

Sometimes all it takes is writing *something*—even if it's wrong. You can tell ChatGPT, "I'm stuck. Write the next scene where my protagonist confronts their mentor—but surprise me." You may not use the whole scene, but a single line or emotional beat might be all you need to find your way forward. The goal isn't perfection. It's movement.

If your problem is that your characters feel like they've stopped growing, ChatGPT can help uncover buried potential. Try asking, "What's a fear this character hasn't admitted to yet?" or "How could this character betray someone without realizing it's a betrayal?" Emotional twists like these can reignite interest in the arc and steer the plot back toward something meaningful.

You can also use the midway point to deepen theme. Maybe you've lost your way because your story has become about plot mechanics instead of emotional truth. Ask ChatGPT, "What thematic question has been building in this story so far, and how might I make it explicit without turning it into a lecture?" Or ask for metaphor: "Give me a symbolic moment that reflects the protagonist's inner conflict using the setting of 15th-century Florence." These prompts don't just restart writing—they refocus it.

Don't forget, you can workshop dialogue, too. Sometimes just hearing your characters speak again can shake loose what's stuck. Ask ChatGPT to write a heated argument, a confession, a moment of silence between two people who can't say what they really feel. Even if the words aren't quite right, they'll help you remember what the scene is trying to say.

And if the issue is momentum—if things just feel slow or flat—then ask for chaos. "What is the worst thing that could happen to this character right now that would force them to act?" or "What historical event could suddenly explode into this quiet village and destroy the status quo?" Escalation is a great way to jolt a story back to life.

When you're writing historical drama, the middle can feel like a swamp of detail, tension, and half-resolved threads. But it's also the place where your characters are most alive. They've made choices, crossed lines, and now they're dealing with it. They're no longer who they were at the start—but they're not yet who they're going to become. That's powerful. That's messy. That's *human*. And that's where your story can dig in and find real emotional gold.

So when you're stuck, don't panic. Break the problem down. Ask specific questions. Try weird ideas. Let ChatGPT throw you some unexpected scenes. And keep the conversation going—between you and the story, between your characters and their world, and between you and the quiet voice inside that still knows what this story is about.

Because getting stuck isn't the end. It's a turning point. And with the right push, it becomes the place where the story truly begins to sing.

Writing Opening Scenes That Transport Instantly

The first scene in a historical drama has a big job. It has to transport the reader or viewer immediately—not just to a place, but to a *time*. It has to say: this isn't now, this isn't today, but it's still human, still alive, still worth your attention. The moment your story opens, you're building a bridge between the past and the present. And if you get it right, that bridge is invisible. The reader doesn't even feel the crossing. They're just *there*—inside the moment, breathing the air, hearing the voices, seeing the world through a different lens.

But how do you actually do that? How do you write an opening scene that doesn't feel like a history lesson, a museum exhibit, or a slow march through exposition?

It starts with **immersive detail**, but not just *any* detail. You don't need to rattle off the year, the ruling monarch, the political climate, and the fashions of the day in the first paragraph. You need to *anchor the reader inside a moment that feels alive*. That means choosing *specific*, *sensory*, *emotional* elements that hint at the larger world without dumping it on the reader all at once.

Imagine you're writing a story set in 14th-century Florence. Don't start with, "The year was 1348 and the Black Death was sweeping through Europe." Start with a boy stealing a loaf of bread from a dying vendor whose open sores are bleeding onto the cobblestones. Let us smell the smoke from the baker's chimney, hear the church bell tolling not for time but for death, and watch the boy hesitate before running. We don't need the history spelled out—we *feel* it.

Ask ChatGPT for scene prompts like, "Write the opening to a story set in plague-ridden Florence through the eyes of a child thief." You'll get not just setting, but atmosphere and character woven together in a way that instantly places us inside the world.

Another approach is to open on **a moment of tension**, even if it's small. A woman hiding a letter. A man realizing the guards are at the door. A servant overhearing a name they shouldn't have heard. Tension hooks attention, and attention leads the audience forward. It doesn't have to be explosive—it just has to feel *loaded* with unspoken consequences.

Use ChatGPT to generate options: "Give me five tense historical opening scenes involving a secret being discovered," or "Create a scene where a character witnesses something they shouldn't during a royal procession in 18th-century France." These are not exposition—they're invitations into a world already in motion.

Characters matter just as much as setting. In the opening scene, we don't need to know your protagonist's entire backstory. But we do need a *window into their world*. We need to understand what they see, what they fear, what they want—even if they can't articulate it yet. Open with *a feeling*, not a fact. A woman running barefoot down a hallway. A man gripping a sword he never meant to use. A child whispering a prayer before stealing into the night.

Let ChatGPT help you shape that emotional entry point: "Describe the thoughts of a runaway bride in 1800s New England as she slips out the back door on her wedding day," or "Write a short internal monologue from a young soldier about to fight his first battle in the Crimean War."

You can also start with **ritual or routine**—something that shows what daily life is like for your character in their time. The way they dress, pray, eat, speak to their family, or prepare for a task can quietly establish the world's rules. But within that routine, something should be *off*. The best opening scenes hint that this isn't just another day. It's the beginning of change. A routine that will be interrupted. A normal that won't last.

ChatGPT can brainstorm these layered scenes with you: "Give me a scene of a woman preparing bread in a Roman villa just before learning of her husband's death," or "Describe a samurai's morning ritual before discovering he's been betrayed by his clan."

Dialogue can work beautifully in an opening—*if* it reveals something. A servant muttering under her breath about her mistress's cruelty. A schoolteacher correcting a student while hiding his own fear of the secret police. Let the way people speak tell us what they're *afraid to say*. Language, tone, and silence all build the texture of time.

You can ask ChatGPT for historically tuned dialogue: "Write a short exchange between two palace maids in Imperial Russia gossiping about a scandal," or "Create a tense dialogue between a medieval priest and a grieving father." The goal isn't to sound perfect—it's to sound *lived in*.

And then there's atmosphere. The weather, the lighting, the feel of the air—all of it matters. Historical drama lives in the mood. Fog rolling across a battlefield. Rain dripping off iron gates. Dust in a dry market square. These sensory details, when attached to action or emotion, are what make the world feel real. Not the date. Not the facts. The *texture*.

When in doubt, try this prompt: "Give me an atmospheric historical opening set in a desert village at dusk during the early Ottoman Empire." From there, adjust the voice and tone to match your story's pace and themes.

Finally, think of your opening scene as a promise. You're telling the reader: *This is the world. This is the tone. This is what matters here.* It sets expectations for emotion, scale, and pace. So ask yourself, what kind of story am I telling? If it's tragic, let that bleed into the opening. If it's romantic, let us glimpse the ache. If it's political, let us feel the tension before we know the game.

And if you're stuck, just ask ChatGPT: "Write five emotionally resonant first lines for a historical drama about forbidden love in wartime," or "Give me a slow-burn opening that hints at revolution brewing in 1700s Paris." You don't have to use them word-for-word. But they'll get you started. Because the goal of your opening isn't to explain. It's to *transport*. To pull the reader by the heart into a world that no longer exists—but still matters. And when you get that right, you don't need to convince them to keep reading.

They're already there.

Writing Endings That Echo Across Time

A great ending doesn't just close a story—it reverberates. It lingers in the mind like smoke after a fire, like silence after a final word. In historical drama, where your story is grounded in the tension between fact and feeling, your ending carries an added weight. Because you're not just finishing a narrative—you're stepping away from an entire world that really existed. The goal isn't to wrap everything up. It's to leave the reader or viewer *feeling* the passage of time, the weight of choices, the shadow of what's been lost, and the echo of what still matters.

So how do you craft an ending that doesn't just stop—but *resonates*?

The secret lies in creating a final moment that ties the personal to the historical. That means whatever emotional arc your character has gone through must land alongside the greater arc of the world they're part of. The love story, the moral fall, the fight for justice—it all happens inside a world that's also been changing. The best endings show how those changes mirror each other.

Let's say your story is about a midwife in 16th-century France who secretly helps women escape abusive marriages. Maybe her story ends in exile, or death, or quiet obscurity. But the ending isn't about whether she won or lost—it's about whether her choices *meant* something. Did someone live because of her? Did someone remember her name? Did the world shift a little, even if it didn't look like it? That's the emotional echo. That's where endings live.

You can ask ChatGPT for endings that carry this kind of resonance. Try, "What would be a powerful, bittersweet ending for a woman who defied the church during the Reformation?" or "Give me an ending that feels emotionally satisfying for a servant who witnessed a political assassination in 1800s Vienna."

Sometimes the most powerful historical endings are quiet. A man burying a uniform he can no longer wear. A letter never sent. A photograph tucked into a drawer. These small acts carry emotional weight precisely because the world has been so loud around them. The character's silence becomes a kind of rebellion, or peace, or acceptance. Use ChatGPT to help find these moments: "Describe a wordless final scene where a woman says goodbye to the only home she's ever known after war forces her out."

One of the best techniques for creating endings that echo is **cyclical structure**—ending the story where it began, but with everything changed. A child returns to the village they fled. A soldier walks through a street that once held celebration, now ruined. The echo isn't just in the image, but in the emotional shift. Ask ChatGPT, "Create a closing scene that mirrors the opening in a story about a boy who becomes a soldier during Napoleon's fall."

Another powerful ending tool is **legacy**. Especially in historical drama, where lives are so often dictated by systems outside their control, what matters most is what survives the character. Did their child learn from their mistakes? Did their letters reach someone who needed them? Did the secret they kept come to light years later and change someone's life? The character may be gone—but the *impact* remains.

You might ask, "What would be a good legacy-driven ending for a character who smuggled banned literature in Stalin's Russia?" or "Write a final scene in which a grandchild uncovers the truth about their ancestor's role in a rebellion." These echoes across generations deepen the emotional resonance and remind the reader that the past isn't really past. It's still unfolding through us.

Don't be afraid of endings that are *ambiguous*—so long as they feel earned. In history, closure is rare. Sometimes the most truthful ending is the one that leaves a question hanging in the air. Will the revolution work? Will the lovers reunite? Will justice ever come? Ask ChatGPT to explore ambiguity: "Write an emotionally charged ending that leaves the reader uncertain whether a character survived a purge in 1970s Argentina." The uncertainty, if rooted in truth, can be far more haunting than a clean resolution.

The best endings also carry a *thematic echo*. If your story is about identity, end with a character choosing who they are—quietly or defiantly. If it's about power, show what's left when the power structure collapses. If it's about memory, let someone remember something the world tried to erase. Use ChatGPT to sharpen these emotional beats: "Give me a closing image that reinforces a theme of generational sacrifice in a story set during the Partition of India."

Sometimes a single line can carry the entire weight of the ending. A whispered apology. A name spoken for the first time. A realization that arrives too late. These lines stick. You can ask ChatGPT for closing dialogue options: "Write a final sentence for a man realizing the war he fought for meant nothing," or "Give me a closing line that suggests hope after loss in a 19th-century frontier town."

Finally, don't underestimate the power of *symbolism*. A clock stopping. A candle going out. A church bell ringing. The birth of a child. The ringing of a ship's bell. These moments create a final image that locks into the reader's memory. And the stronger your image, the more the emotion will echo long after the page is turned. Try asking, "Suggest five symbolic final moments that reflect freedom and grief," or "What's a visually rich final moment for a character walking away from a battlefield?"

Because at the end of the story, it's not the historical date we remember. It's the feeling. The silence that falls when the last words are said. The air around a character's final choice. The way the past settles into the present and refuses to be forgotten.

When you write an ending that echoes across time, you're not just finishing a story.

You're reminding us that the past is still breathing, still reaching forward, still asking to be understood.

And that's a powerful place to leave your reader standing. Quiet. Changed. And still listening.

Playing With Power: Authority, Rebellion, and Control

Historical drama is built on power—who has it, who wants it, who abuses it, and who tries to take it back. Whether your story is set in a palace, a prison, a battlefield, or a village, there's always a tension between those in charge and those who aren't. And when that tension becomes personal—when authority clashes with rebellion, when control slips or is seized—your story comes alive. Because power is never just about kings and empires. It's about fathers and daughters, landowners and laborers, priests and outcasts. It's about the decisions that make people tremble, bow, rise, or break.

Writing about power in historical drama means understanding that it's *everywhere*. It lives in the words characters can or cannot say. It shows up in body language, silence, rules, ritual, and inherited fear. A servant who hesitates before speaking. A noble who demands obedience without looking up. A slave who can't look someone in the eye. These moments show power more vividly than a coronation or a courtroom.

To explore power on the page, start by identifying your power structure. Who is officially in charge? What institutions, beliefs, or traditions uphold their authority? Is it monarchy, military, religion, gender, caste, class, or race? Often, it's a combination of these forces. Once you know who holds the reins, then look at who is trapped beneath them—and how that pressure cooks your characters into action.

Ask ChatGPT to help you clarify this setup. Try: "Describe the power structure of a feudal Japanese household and the tensions between samurai and servants," or "What forms of informal authority might exist among enslaved people on a Caribbean plantation in the 1700s?" This groundwork helps you understand the invisible forces shaping your characters' lives.

Next, ask how your characters *respond* to power. Do they enforce it? Resist it? Subvert it quietly? Try to survive within it? Each character has a different relationship to control. A general might use war to keep control of his men, but feel helpless against his own king. A queen might wield power publicly while being emotionally manipulated behind closed doors. A teenage girl might rebel against her father's expectations—but be trapped by society's deeper rules.

Power becomes drama when it becomes *personal*. When someone who's supposed to obey says no. When someone who's meant to lead hesitates. When a rule is broken not for politics, but for love, justice, survival, or revenge. These moments of defiance or submission define who your characters are. Ask ChatGPT for help creating these reversals: "Give me a scene where a kitchen maid blackmails a noble for her brother's freedom," or "Write a confrontation between a young revolutionary and his former mentor who now serves the crown."

One of the most interesting things you can do in historical drama is to blur the lines between authority and rebellion. What happens when the rebel becomes the tyrant? When the servant begins to manipulate the master? When the hero has to enforce the very rules they once fought against? Power corrupts—but it also transforms. And characters who shift between sides—willingly or not—create the kind of complexity that keeps audiences hooked.

Power also works in *subtle* ways. A servant pouring tea can control the mood of the room by how they move. A wife in a patriarchal society can control her husband's reputation with a single word at a dinner party. A child can destroy a legacy by telling a secret. These aren't grand rebellions, but they are deeply human moments of control, and they reveal that no one is ever entirely powerless.

You can ask ChatGPT to help with these micro-conflicts: "What small but impactful act of rebellion could a governess perform in 1850s London without being caught?" or "How might a monk in a silent order resist authority without ever speaking?" These kinds of choices build tension while staying true to the constraints of the setting.

If you're writing about a large-scale rebellion—a peasant uprising, a revolution, a coup—remember that those movements are made of individual lives. The people fighting don't always agree. Some want justice. Some want revenge. Some want power for themselves. That's where your drama lives—in the cracks within the cause. Ask ChatGPT, "What internal conflicts might split a group of female textile workers during a labor strike in 19th-century Manchester?" or "How could a betrayal within a slave rebellion change the course of the uprising?"

Ritual is another tool for exploring power. The way people kneel, eat, speak, worship, marry, or bury their dead can all reflect who's in control. A character who interrupts or alters a ritual—deliberately or accidentally—can send shockwaves through the story. You can use ChatGPT to help imagine these dynamics: "Describe a traditional ceremony in a fictional Eastern European village where outsiders are forbidden to speak," or "What happens if a knight refuses to bow during a coronation in medieval England?"

Symbols of power—clothing, seals, weapons, documents, relics—can also shift hands during a story. A crown stolen. A letter forged. A robe torn. These objects carry narrative weight. They change the balance. They speak without words. Ask ChatGPT, "What objects would symbolize power in an ancient Persian court?" or "What item could be used as leverage against a corrupt bishop in 1500s France?"

And remember—power always has a cost. Whether it's taken, lost, protected, or shared, it leaves a mark. A character who climbs to power may lose the people they love. A character who fights for freedom may find themselves alone when victory comes. A character who stays silent to survive may lose the ability to speak their truth at all. These consequences are what give your story depth and emotional weight.

When you write historical drama with power in focus, you're not just telling stories of kings and rebels. You're telling stories of people navigating systems they didn't create. People trying to protect themselves, their families, or their beliefs in a world that often doesn't care what they want.

So let your characters push against those systems. Let them break the rules, or follow them bitterly. Let them rise, fall, suffer, and surprise themselves.

Because power isn't static—it's a storm. And in historical drama, the ones caught inside it are the ones we remember most.

How Historical Norms Shape Character Decisions

One of the most powerful forces in historical drama isn't war, weather, or fate—it's the invisible rules. The expectations. The beliefs that say, *This is how things are, this is who you're allowed to be, this is what you must do.* These are the historical norms—the cultural, legal, religious, and moral boundaries that shape every character's world. And if you're writing a compelling historical story, you need to let those norms breathe through your characters. Because no one makes decisions in a vacuum. We're all shaped by the world we live in—and your characters should be, too.

Historical norms are often what keep your characters trapped. They're the reason a woman can't inherit land. The reason a man can't love another man openly. The reason a child can be married off at twelve, or a servant can be beaten for speaking out. And they're not just rules—they're internalized. That's what makes them so emotionally complex. Your character may not even realize they have a choice. Or if they do, the cost of making that choice might be unthinkable.

This is where deep drama lives. In the tension between what a character *wants* and what they're *allowed* to want.

Take, for example, a young woman in 1700s Puritan New England who wants to become a healer. She might not consciously think, *I'm breaking the rules.* She might just feel drawn to the natural world, to herbs, to knowledge passed down from her grandmother. But the cultural norm says, *that's witchcraft.* So every decision she makes—every time she helps someone, hides her tools, or even speaks with confidence—carries weight. It's dangerous. It's defiant. And it tells us who she is in a way no exposition ever could.

Ask ChatGPT to help you map these tensions: "What taboos would a female midwife face in 17th-century England?" or "How might a man raised in a strict Catholic village in 1920s Spain respond to discovering his son is gay?" The answers reveal not just plot opportunities—but layers of emotional conflict.

It's important to remember that norms aren't just obstacles. They're also the *default operating system* of the character's mind. A nobleman in ancient Rome might not question slavery because it's the air he breathes. A Confucian scholar in imperial China might genuinely believe that obedience is a moral duty. A plantation owner's daughter in 19th-century America might feel guilt—but still accept the structure that gives her comfort. These characters don't have to be villains—they just live in a system that hasn't taught them to see it any other way. Until something changes.

And that's where drama enters. The moment a character begins to *see differently*, even a little, their choices start to shift. Maybe they read a banned book. Maybe they fall in love with someone forbidden. Maybe they see injustice with their own eyes. That shift in perception—the slow burn of *what if they're wrong*—is where some of the best historical character arcs begin.

You can explore this with ChatGPT by asking, "What would make a loyal member of a royal court begin to question their king during a famine?" or "What experience might make a noblewoman support a peasant revolt in 18th-century France?" The key is to find the moment where the norm cracks—and a human being begins to wrestle with something bigger than themselves.

But not all characters will rebel. Some will cling to the norms even as they suffer. A woman might stay in a loveless marriage because duty is more powerful than desire. A soldier might follow orders he hates because disobedience would bring shame to his family. These characters may not be heroes—but they're real. And when you write them with empathy, they become unforgettable.

Historical norms also help create *social tension* between characters. A freed Black man speaking to a white aristocrat in Reconstruction-era America. A Jewish tailor serving a Nazi officer in 1930s Berlin. A widow trying to manage her late husband's estate in 1600s Italy while male relatives question her every decision. These are not just character interactions—they are acts of defiance, survival, compromise, or endurance. Ask ChatGPT, "What kind of social tension would exist between a Japanese noble and a merchant in feudal Japan?" or "How might a suffragette and her conservative sister clash during the early 1900s?"

Norms don't always come from governments or religions. They live in families, in communities, in the unspoken rituals of daily life. A daughter might fear breaking her mother's heart more than breaking the law. A son might marry for politics instead of love because it's what's expected. The more specific and personal the norm, the more powerful the drama when it's challenged.

Symbols and rituals also carry the weight of these norms. A girl putting on a wedding dress she didn't choose. A man refusing to kneel before a king. A child being taught which words are forbidden. These are moments of cultural expectation made visible—and they speak volumes. You can ask ChatGPT, "What ritual might represent a young boy's induction into manhood in 15th-century Africa?" or "What traditional expectation might a widow break by refusing to remarry in 18th-century India?"

And the most important thing to remember? Your character doesn't have to explain the norm to the reader. They just have to *feel it*. The fear. The guilt. The pride. The quiet resignation. The longing to be free. These emotions carry the truth of the time, and they let your audience feel the weight of history without needing a lecture.

Because in historical drama, the best character decisions don't just move the plot—they reveal the time period through emotion, conflict, and sacrifice. And when a character chooses to challenge—or obey—a historical norm, we see not just who they are, but who we are too.

That's the magic. You're not just writing the past. You're writing the past *as it was lived*—one difficult, courageous, conflicted decision at a time.

Showing Social Class through Conflict and Detail

In historical drama, social class isn't just background noise—it's a living, breathing presence that shapes every interaction, decision, and unspoken rule. Class defines where a character sleeps, what they wear, how they speak, and who they're allowed to love or defy. It can be rigid or fluid, enforced through laws or tradition, worn proudly or hidden in shame. But most of all, it creates *conflict*. And it's through that conflict—and the subtle details that support it—that social class becomes something the audience feels, not just understands.

You don't have to start with a revolution or an uprising to explore class. In fact, the most compelling moments are often quiet. A servant who pauses before sitting down. A noble who hesitates before shaking someone's hand. A merchant who wears silk to a dinner where cotton would be more appropriate. These small, telling details build a sense of structure—and tension—without any explanation. You show the divide instead of telling us about it.

Ask ChatGPT for help building these details: "What are subtle social cues a servant in 18th-century Vienna would observe when entering a noble's home?" or "What small signals would indicate wealth or status among fishermen in 1800s coastal Japan?" These questions help you create believable class distinctions that go beyond clichés.

Language is another powerful tool. People speak differently across class lines—not just in accent or vocabulary, but in *what* they say and *how* they say it. A noble might speak in layered implication, trained in diplomacy. A working-class character might speak plainly—or not at all—because being outspoken could be dangerous. Class-based dialogue can reveal power dynamics in every sentence. Ask ChatGPT to write dialogue examples: "Give me a short exchange between a Victorian factory owner and a child laborer," or "Show how a knight addresses a queen in public versus in private."

Clothing, of course, plays a key role in signaling class. But it's not just about finery versus rags. A wealthy widow in mourning black. A soldier in a borrowed coat. A maid with one good dress saved for feast days. These details say everything about who they are, what they've lost, and what they're trying to protect. Let the clothing *mean* something. You can prompt ChatGPT: "Describe the clothing of a minor noble who's recently fallen into debt in 17th-century France," or "What would a successful merchant wear to try and pass as upper class in Renaissance Italy?"

Social class also defines physical space. Who gets the corner room with the window? Who sleeps in the attic? Who enters through the front door, and who uses the servant's entrance? Class defines not just where people go, but what they're allowed to *see*. Think of a castle—do your characters live in the grand halls or scrub the floors beneath them? Use ChatGPT to map out these hierarchies: "What rooms in a 19th-century manor house would be off-limits to staff?" or "How would a poor family's home in post-war London be structured compared to a middle-class home?"

Now, let's talk about *conflict*. Social class creates natural dramatic friction. A servant who overhears too much. A noble falling in love with someone beneath them. A middle-class clerk trying to rise too fast and stepping on the wrong toes. These conflicts are powerful not just because they're personal—but because they challenge the system itself. A character breaking a class boundary isn't just risking shame—they might be risking everything.

ChatGPT can help you brainstorm these setups: "What social consequences would a duke's daughter face for marrying a blacksmith in 1500s England?" or "What tension might arise if a former slave rises to a position of leadership in post-Civil War America?" These stories are rooted in the time period—but they carry modern emotional resonance, too.

Don't underestimate the power of internalized class. A character doesn't need an enemy to feel the pressure of social hierarchy—they can carry it inside. A maid might refuse to sit in a chair, even when alone. A poor scholar might downplay their knowledge around nobles. A footman might stand straighter in borrowed clothes, not because anyone's watching, but because he wants to *belong*. This self-policing creates an emotional realism that deepens every scene.

You can ask ChatGPT for psychological nuance: "Describe the inner monologue of a laundress invited to a wedding at the manor where she works," or "How might a self-made merchant struggle with imposter syndrome at a royal event?" These kinds of reflections make class feel like more than just economics—it becomes identity.

Even relationships are shaped by class. A love affair between a noble and a servant is never just about love—it's about risk, power imbalance, and a hundred unspoken consequences. A friendship between a soldier and a general's son might falter when war ends and social roles reassert themselves. A father's ambition might drive a child into a world where they no longer feel at home. Let these emotional crosscurrents build your scenes from the inside out.

Ritual and etiquette can also expose class conflict. Who speaks first at the table? Who gets served last? Who bows deeper, and who pretends not to see the slight? Ask ChatGPT: "Describe a formal dinner in 19th-century Russia and how class dynamics play out through behavior," or "What are five ways a lower-class character might subtly rebel during a church service in medieval England?" The answers can form the backbone of key scenes.

Class also influences how characters imagine their future. A servant may dream only of a better position in the household—not of owning land. A noble might fear scandal more than death. A merchant might see money as freedom, but never quite gain acceptance from those born into power. These internal limitations—these inherited ceilings—can be more powerful than any external obstacle.

So when you write historical drama, let class seep into every crack. Not just in plot, but in gesture, silence, architecture, food, scent, voice, and gaze. Let your characters climb, fall, hide, or fight—but always within the pressures of where they stand and what the world allows them to reach for.

Because the story of social class is the story of permission—who has it, who gives it, who takes it back. And when you show it through the subtle language of conflict and detail, your historical world stops being a setting.

It becomes real. And unforgettable.

Using Historical Symbols for Emotional Weight

Symbols are the quiet giants of historical drama. They don't shout. They don't rush. But when used with intention, they carry an emotional weight that can echo through an entire story. In historical settings, symbols are everywhere—woven into flags, rituals, uniforms, heirlooms, architecture, religion, and even superstition. They tell us who belongs, who rules, who rebels, who remembers, and who must forget. But more importantly, they tell us what *matters*—not just to a time period, but to a character. And when something symbolic is broken, stolen, hidden, or reclaimed, that emotional impact can hit harder than any plot twist.

To use symbols well in historical drama, you first need to understand their *cultural power*. A rosary during the Spanish Inquisition is not just a piece of jewelry. A red armband in 1940s Germany is not just fabric. A family crest burned during a peasant revolt is not just fire—it's identity lost, erased, or rewritten. These objects carry history, but they also carry *feeling*—shame, pride, fear, hope. When a character touches or reacts to a symbol, it reveals their internal world without a word spoken.

Start by anchoring your story in a few powerful symbols that are tied directly to your characters. Maybe a soldier wears a torn flag around his arm like a bandage. Maybe a noblewoman locks a bloodstained coronet in a box and never opens it again. Maybe a former slave buries the papers declaring his freedom because they no longer feel true. These symbols don't need to be obvious. Their power comes from their *emotional meaning*.

Ask ChatGPT for help crafting these elements. You can prompt, "What personal item might a soldier in Napoleon's army carry that represents both loyalty and loss?" or "Give me a symbolic object for a woman accused of witchcraft in 1600s Scotland that she refuses to let go of." The answers might give you more than props—they might unlock a whole emotional thread.

Symbolism becomes especially potent when it *changes*. A symbol that begins with one meaning and ends with another tells a complete arc without spelling it out. A wedding ring becomes a weight after betrayal. A royal seal becomes a lie after a coup. A sword once wielded for glory becomes a burden carried in silence. These reversals give your story texture and emotional honesty.

Symbols can also tie characters together—or drive them apart. Think of a family heirloom passed down through generations. A letter never delivered. A medal earned but never worn. When one character understands the meaning of a symbol and another does not, it creates tension, secrecy, or grief. Ask ChatGPT, "What object might be used to quietly pass rebellion messages during the French Resistance?" or "How could a piece of jewelry become a source of shame in a Victorian family scandal?"

You can use symbols as anchors in your story—objects or images that appear at key moments, marking emotional shifts. A candle burning during a secret meeting. A bell that tolls for each execution. A piece of clothing that changes hands. Each reappearance adds weight. Readers and viewers begin to recognize the object not just for what it is, but for what it *represents*. And in a historical world, where personal expression is often constrained, these symbols speak louder than characters ever could.

Even setting can become symbolic. A crumbling church. A locked garden. A bridge no one crosses. These are spaces that hold memory, tradition, trauma, or hope. You can ask ChatGPT to help build these: "What symbolic locations might appear in a story set during the Russian Revolution?" or "Give me a recurring setting in 19th-century Ireland that represents both oppression and community." These places can become almost characters themselves, offering emotional shorthand that deepens the world.

Another powerful technique is using *religious or political symbols* in personal ways. A character might deface a statue, not as an act of rebellion but as a form of grief. A priest might hide a sacred relic out of guilt. A revolutionary might carry the emblem of the regime he now fights against. These moments remind us that even the most public symbols are carried privately. They mean different things to different people—and that contradiction creates rich emotional drama.

Don't forget that even *natural symbols* can carry historical weight. A withered tree in a battlefield. A flock of birds leaving a burning city. A river that once marked a border now running dry. Nature often reflects the internal world of your characters, especially when paired with history. These images stay with readers because they transcend language—they feel timeless, even when deeply rooted in the past.

Ask ChatGPT for poetic moments: "Describe a symbolic natural event that reflects the loss of innocence in a medieval coming-of-age story," or "Give me a visual metaphor for the collapse of a family dynasty in 18th-century China." These moments give your narrative a heartbeat that goes beyond facts and into emotion.

The most important thing about symbols in historical drama is *intimacy*. Anyone can recognize a crown or a flag. But when you make a symbol personal—when it means something to one character in a way no one else quite understands—it becomes unforgettable. A single coin. A burned book. A handkerchief sewn with initials. These are the moments readers carry with them long after the final page.

So don't be afraid to let objects carry weight. Let them pass through hands, cross borders, witness change. Let them break, or be hidden, or be found again. Let your characters hold on to them too tightly, or let them go too soon. Let them say what no one can say.

Because when you use historical symbols well, they do more than decorate the world—they speak for it. They remember what was lost. They honor what was endured. And they show us, in quiet, devastating detail, that history is not just made of events.

It's made of what people *couldn't let go of.*

ChatGPT as Your Brainstorming Partner

Writing historical drama can feel like dragging a heavy, beautiful tapestry across a crowded room. You've got the weight of history, the complexity of human emotion, the burden of accuracy, and the demand for good storytelling all pressing in at once. Some days you're full of fire, pulling scene after scene out of the ether. Other days, it's like your mind is fogged over, and even your best ideas sound like half-formed echoes. That's where ChatGPT comes in—not as a replacement for your creativity, but as a reliable, tireless brainstorming partner who never needs sleep, coffee, or compliments.

The beauty of using ChatGPT at the brainstorming stage is that you don't need polished ideas. You don't even need clarity. All you need is curiosity. You can come in with a vague feeling—"I want to write something set during the fall of Constantinople, but I don't know whose story to tell"—and walk away with character sketches, relationship dynamics, possible twists, and emotional hooks that you wouldn't have found on your own. The key is to *talk to ChatGPT like you'd talk to a co-writer*. Be open, messy, spontaneous.

Let's say you've got the seed of a scene: a young girl hiding during a massacre. That's it. You can prompt ChatGPT with, "Help me brainstorm five different reasons why this girl might be significant to the larger story." Or, "What could this character overhear that changes the course of the plot?" Instead of spending hours circling the problem, you're feeding your story oxygen in seconds.

Character creation is one of the best ways to use ChatGPT. You don't always want a perfect protagonist on day one. Sometimes, you want options. You can say, "Give me three types of characters who might have lived in 15th-century Florence and carried emotional secrets," or "Help me brainstorm a historical character who starts out as a coward but grows into a quiet revolutionary." ChatGPT will return ideas that might surprise you—or stir something in your own imagination that takes you in a completely different direction.

You can also use it to explore the *what-ifs* that fuel good historical fiction. "What if a servant in Versailles witnessed something that could ruin the royal family?" "What if a plague doctor fell in love with a patient?" "What if a World War I deserter forged a new identity and was blackmailed decades later?" ChatGPT can run with those ideas, throwing you setups, motivations, and potential consequences that you can tweak or reject until the story feels like yours.

One of the most effective brainstorming moves is working backwards. You might know how you want the story to end—let's say your character dies anonymously but is later honored as a hero. Ask ChatGPT, "What series of events might lead to this ending in a story set during the fall of the Berlin Wall?" It will start giving you a roadmap, and you can customize it until it feels emotionally and thematically aligned with your vision.

You don't need to ask only big questions. Sometimes the details can be overwhelming, and brainstorming those with ChatGPT saves hours of stress. You can say, "Give me a few meaningful but subtle ways a character could show guilt in a 1930s church setting," or "What's a poetic way to describe frost gathering on a battlefield at dawn?" You're not just brainstorming plot—you're brainstorming *texture, mood, emotion.*

And if you get stuck—really stuck—you can turn the problem into a conversation. Say something like, "Here's what I've written so far. I feel like the tension dropped off in the middle. Can you help me think through where to take it next?" ChatGPT can point out missed opportunities, deepen your character arcs, or suggest ways to escalate conflict organically.

It's also a brilliant tool for breaking routines. If you find yourself writing the same type of characters, the same kind of scenes, or falling into predictable pacing, you can ask ChatGPT for disruption. "What would be an unexpected but historically believable twist in a story about a monk during the Spanish Inquisition?" or "Give me three ways to introduce a new character who immediately shifts the emotional tone of the story." You'll get answers that challenge your instincts—and that's where fresh storytelling lives.

Even world-building can benefit from AI brainstorming. If you're not quite sure how to describe a medieval port city at night or a grand feast in a Moroccan palace, ChatGPT can fill in those blanks with researched, vivid description that you can adjust to suit your tone. Don't hesitate to say, "Make it darker, more mysterious," or "Add political tension under the surface." You're not taking what it gives you blindly—you're shaping it like clay.

Another great use of ChatGPT is generating symbolic layers. You might say, "Help me brainstorm five historical symbols that could reflect a character's emotional journey," or "Give me objects that could carry deep meaning for someone living through the Irish famine." These become threads you can weave into the narrative, enriching your themes without weighing down your story.

And when doubt creeps in—as it always does—use ChatGPT to hype your idea back up. "Why might this story about a disillusioned war nurse in 1917 matter to modern readers?" You'll get back reasons rooted in human experience, universal struggle, resilience, and justice. Sometimes you need a creative partner who can remind you why the story *matters*.

So don't just think of ChatGPT as a tool for checking spelling or fixing clunky dialogue. Think of it as a mirror, a muse, a brainstorming partner who never gets tired of your questions, never rolls its eyes at your weirdest ideas, and never says, "That's been done before." It's there to help you take the weight off your shoulders just enough so your creativity can breathe.

Because you've still got to write the story—but you don't have to build it alone.

Using Real Quotes to Anchor Fiction

Historical fiction walks a beautiful tightrope between imagination and authenticity. You're creating characters who never lived, conversations that never happened, emotions and relationships that are entirely your invention—but you're placing them in a world shaped by real events. And sometimes, a single line—a sentence someone truly spoke or wrote—can pin your whole story to the historical ground like a nail through silk. A well-placed real quote doesn't just make your fiction feel real. It gives your story gravity. It invites the reader to stop and think, *Someone actually said that. This really happened.* And suddenly, everything feels more alive.

Using real quotes in historical drama is one of the most powerful ways to add emotional weight, thematic resonance, or historical context—without ever having to break the flow of your story. It lets the voices of the past whisper inside your fiction, adding texture, authority, and sometimes even poetry.

So how do you use real quotes effectively?

Start by thinking about *why* a quote belongs in your scene. Are you anchoring a moment in a specific historical time? Are you layering theme or symbolism? Are you giving a character a worldview shaped by their environment? Maybe your character is about to make a choice that parallels something a real person once said. You're not quoting for accuracy alone—you're quoting to *connect.*

For example, if your story is set during the French Revolution, and a character is facing execution, you might have them reflect on the famous final words of Georges Danton: "Show my head to the people. It is worth seeing." That line doesn't need to be spoken aloud. It could be remembered. Echoed. Mutated into a private thought. The quote becomes a tether to the historical moment, but also a mirror for your fictional character's courage—or fear.

You can use ChatGPT to find relevant quotes for your scene. Try prompts like, "Give me powerful last words spoken by historical figures during the French Revolution," or "Share quotes from letters written by soldiers during World War I." You'll get words you can use directly, paraphrase, or let your characters reflect on in their own way.

Sometimes a quote works beautifully as a thematic *bookend.* Open your story with a quote that encapsulates the era's worldview—a line from a philosopher, a monarch, a preacher, or a poet. Then, by the end, echo that quote through your characters, either to reaffirm or subvert it. For instance, if your story begins with the quote, "Those who cannot remember the past are condemned to repeat it," you might show a character living through the same mistakes generations later—but choosing differently.

Another method is embedding quotes into your character's worldview. Let them reference texts, speeches, or cultural sayings that shaped their upbringing. A schoolboy in Nazi Germany might recite lines from Hitler Youth propaganda. A suffragette in 1900s England might draw inspiration from Mary Wollstonecraft or Emmeline Pankhurst. A soldier during the American Civil War might carry a letter quoting Abraham Lincoln. The quote becomes part of their emotional DNA.

These quotes can also function as emotional triggers. A character might remember something their parent once said—a phrase that's been passed down. Maybe they repeat it in moments of stress. Maybe they hate it. Maybe it shapes the way they see themselves. You can ask ChatGPT to help generate these connections: "What are some religious or patriotic quotes that might be passed down in 19th-century Irish Catholic families?" or "What quote might a child growing up in Stalinist Russia hear in school that would shape their belief in authority?"

Not all quotes need to be famous. Sometimes the most powerful lines come from obscure documents—old letters, trial transcripts, personal diaries. These give your story the feel of something discovered. They bring in the raw voice of history—not polished, not performative, but real. And when you put those raw voices beside your fictional ones, the contrast can be electric.

Ask ChatGPT, "Give me excerpts from letters written by Civil War nurses," or "Find quotes from 19th-century miners describing working conditions." You might use the quote directly in a character's letter. Or have them paraphrase it. Or deny it. Either way, the real quote grounds the scene and adds historical depth.

Sometimes quotes aren't spoken at all. They're *seen*. On posters. On banners. In pamphlets or graffiti. These are especially powerful in stories about resistance, propaganda, or political transformation. "Arbeit macht frei" at the gates of Auschwitz says more than pages of exposition. "Liberté, égalité, fraternité" scrawled across a ruined wall in Paris can turn into a haunting reminder of broken dreams. A character seeing such a line—painted, burned, etched—can spark a memory, a betrayal, or a promise. Use ChatGPT to find these: "What slogans were used by protesters in 1968 France?" or "What inscriptions were common in anti-slavery tracts during the abolition movement?"

Quotes can also be used ironically. A character might cling to a saying like "God helps those who help themselves" in a world where that clearly isn't true. Or a leader might quote something noble while acting cruelly—forcing your audience to see the gap between words and actions. This irony deepens your storytelling and reminds the reader that history is always complicated.

And of course, you can fictionalize the use of quotes too. A character might misquote a famous line, or misinterpret it. They might mock it, twist it, weaponize it. Letting your fictional characters *interact* with real historical language makes your world feel layered, living, and full of tension.

A good rule of thumb: use quotes the way a composer uses musical motifs. Let them return. Let them evolve. Let them carry memory and meaning. One well-placed quote, whispered at the climax or remembered in the final line, can leave a mark that lasts longer than any action scene.

So whether you're pulling from speeches, diaries, manifestos, graffiti, or grave markers, don't be afraid to let real words enter your fictional world. They don't distract—they deepen. They don't take away from your voice—they give it resonance.

Because when your story brushes up against what someone *actually said*, it becomes more than fiction.

It becomes part of the ongoing conversation between the past and the present. A reminder that history isn't just a backdrop.

It's a living echo. And you're one more voice in the chorus.

When to Bend the Truth and When to Keep It Sacred

One of the trickiest—and most liberating—parts of writing historical drama is deciding when to follow the truth and when to let it bend beneath the weight of your story. As a storyteller, you have to walk the line between honoring the past and crafting a compelling narrative. You're not writing a textbook. You're not recreating events frame by frame. You're digging for emotional truth, for human experience. And sometimes, to find that truth, you have to cheat a little on the facts.

So where's the line? When do you stay faithful to history, and when is it okay to rewrite the past?

Start by asking yourself this: what is the *point* of the truth in this moment? Is it giving your story weight? Anchoring the audience in a particular time and place? Honoring real people who lived and died? Or is it simply clutter, a fact for the sake of fact, slowing down a scene that wants to breathe?

Some truths are *sacred*. They shouldn't be touched or twisted lightly. If your story is built around real trauma—a genocide, a massacre, a systemic injustice—then the facts matter. Not just out of respect, but because bending those truths too far does damage. It risks distorting what actually happened and why. If you're writing about slavery, the Holocaust, the Trail of Tears, or any real historical atrocity, you need to do your homework. Understand the context. Use ChatGPT to help research the era, the systems, the survivors. You can ask, "What laws were in place for enslaved people in Virginia in 1800?" or "What testimonies exist from survivors of the Armenian Genocide?" That research shapes how you write, what you choose to show, and what you know not to soften or sensationalize.

When real suffering is involved, keep the core truth sacred. Let your fictional characters exist within it—but don't rewrite history to make it more comfortable. Let the audience feel the weight of what really happened.

But not every part of history is sacred. Sometimes bending the truth is *necessary* to tell a better, sharper, more human story. Maybe a certain event happened in 1867, but you need it to happen in 1871 to match your character's arc. Move it. Maybe a certain law wouldn't realistically be challenged for another decade, but your story needs that act of defiance now. Make it happen. These changes don't erase history—they reshape it into something emotionally and thematically coherent.

Use ChatGPT to help weigh the trade-offs: "What would be the consequences of setting this uprising ten years earlier?" or "Would it be plausible for a woman to secretly own property in this time period if I make her disguise her identity?" These questions keep your story grounded even as you stretch the lines.

A good way to think about bending the truth is to ask whether it helps you get closer to emotional reality. Sometimes the *feelings* are more important than the facts. A composite character who represents a real group of people can sometimes reveal more about the truth of that group than a historically accurate figure ever could. A fictional town set during a real famine can show how communities lived and died without needing to replicate one village exactly.

The key is transparency—with yourself and, when possible, with your audience. If you're bending the truth, know *why* you're doing it. Know what's gained and what's lost. And if your story ever reaches the stage of publication or production, consider including a note explaining what was real and what was imagined. Readers and viewers will appreciate your honesty—and your artistry.

One place where you can bend the truth with great effect is character dialogue. Real people don't always speak in compelling, well-timed lines. That's your job. You can give historical figures sharper voices, clearer motivations, or private thoughts they never shared. Just don't make them say things that completely contradict who they were—unless that contradiction is the point. Ask ChatGPT to help build believable dialogue: "Write a fictional but historically plausible monologue for Marie Antoinette just before her execution," or "Give me a scene where a soldier in the Crimean War expresses doubt in the cause."

You can also take creative liberties with setting. Combine locations. Invent villages. Imagine secret meetings that never happened. These changes don't erase the truth—they focus it. The goal is to create an emotionally immersive experience that honors the world, not just copies it. Ask ChatGPT for ideas like, "What kind of fictional estate could represent the wealth disparity in 18th-century Prussia?" or "Create a believable underground network for smugglers in colonial Boston."

One of the best uses of creative license is to *reclaim forgotten truths*. Maybe you invent a queer love story in a time where such stories were erased. Maybe you write about a woman leading a rebellion, even though records of women in those roles were buried or denied. Sometimes, bending the truth is actually a way of revealing what was once hidden. You can ask ChatGPT, "What are some historically plausible ways a woman might have led soldiers in disguise during the 1600s?" or "How might a Black scholar have secretly circulated radical ideas in 19th-century England?" These stories may not be in the mainstream history books—but they deserve to be told.

And finally, don't let fear of getting everything right freeze your creativity. Historical fiction is a living conversation between fact and imagination. If you've done your research, respected your subjects, and written with clarity and heart, then you've earned the right to shape history into something new. That's not dishonoring the past—it's keeping it alive.

So bend when it deepens the emotion. Stay faithful when it protects the truth. Use your gut and your craft. And remember that the heart of your story is not the date on the page—it's the human being standing in that moment, making a choice that feels real, raw, and unforgettable.

That's the truth that matters most.

Writing a Screenplay from Your Historical Outline

So you've done the hard work. You've outlined your historical drama with care, chosen your time period, developed your characters, shaped your themes, and maybe even finished your novel or a thorough treatment of the story. You've got this rich, dramatic journey laid out from start to finish. Now comes the thrilling shift: turning that beautiful historical outline into a screenplay. And here's where the magic really happens—because screenwriting is where you learn to *show* everything you've built without ever stopping to *explain* it.

Adapting historical material into a screenplay is an act of translation. You're not just retelling events—you're turning them into images, action, and dialogue. You're shedding layers of inner monologue and exposition and leaning instead on moments that live through movement, subtext, silence, and visual storytelling. Screenplays don't ask you to describe the whole world. They ask you to *imply* it—through a look, a gesture, a line of dialogue, or the way a room is lit.

The first step is to take your outline and break it down scene by scene. If your outline already has beats—inciting incident, turning points, climax, resolution—you're halfway there. Each major beat should now become an anchor scene. From those, you'll build the structure of your screenplay. A standard feature film script runs about 100–120 pages, with roughly one page per minute of screen time. For historical drama, that means choosing the most cinematic parts of your story and focusing on what you can *see and hear*.

Let's say your outline starts with a peasant uprising in 1300s France and ends with the fall of a noble house. You might have ten key moments: a rebellion igniting, a forbidden romance, a betrayal in the castle, a murder, a secret revealed, a battle lost, a family fractured, and a final choice. Each of these will become a scene—or a series of scenes—that carries emotional and narrative weight. You can ask ChatGPT, "Help me break this story into 20 key scenes for a two-hour screenplay," and it will help you carve the bones of your story into cinematic moments.

Now, here's where things change from outlining to screenwriting. You can't explain historical context in long paragraphs anymore. The audience won't read your research. They need to feel it. That means starting *in media res*—in the middle of action. You don't begin with a voiceover or a scroll of dates (unless you're really going for a classic epic). You begin with something *visual* that gives us a taste of the world. A woman running through a field of smoke. A priest washing blood from his hands. A noble staring into a mirror as peasants gather outside.

Use ChatGPT to help you shape opening visuals. Try, "What's a striking opening image for a historical drama set in post-Reformation England?" or "Give me a short visual scene to introduce a 16th-century executioner's moral conflict."

Next, adapt your characters for the screen. A novel can tell you what a character thinks. A screenplay must show it. So think about how your characters move, how they react, what they say—and what they leave unsaid. Subtext is your best friend. When a general says, "Hold the line," we should hear the doubt in his voice. When a servant curtsies, the hesitation might say more than the bow itself. Dialogue becomes about conflict, desire, strategy—not exposition.

ChatGPT can help you generate and refine this. You can say, "Write a tense dialogue scene between a noblewoman and her former lover who is now leading a rebellion," or "Create a moment where a character tries to confess guilt without actually saying the words."

Pacing also matters more in screenwriting. Scenes need to move. Dialogue should have rhythm. Action should escalate. And the emotional arc must track visually from beginning to end. Your midpoint should be a twist or a moment of irreversible change. Your climax should be something that can be seen and felt—a battle, a breakdown, a final stand, or a quiet act of rebellion. If your outline says, "This is when she realizes the betrayal," your screenplay must answer: *How do we show that?*

Ask ChatGPT for suggestions like, "How can I show a betrayal between siblings without using dialogue?" or "What visual symbol could reflect a family's fall from power in 19th-century Russia?" These tools help you write visually, not just narratively.

When writing action, don't worry about camera angles unless they're essential. Just describe what we need to *see.* Instead of "The camera pans across the battlefield," say, "Corpses litter the muddy field. A single soldier still breathes, buried in the wreckage." That's the image. Let the director and cinematographer worry about the lens. You focus on the *moment.*

Historical accuracy still matters—but again, it has to be baked into the world without explanation. If your scene takes place in a medieval apothecary, show the tools, the herbs, the symbols, the candles. Let the setting speak. Don't explain it—*live* in it. You can use ChatGPT to enrich these scenes: "Describe the look, smell, and feel of a medieval apothecary where a secret potion is being brewed," or "What would a 19th-century Russian prison look and sound like on the day of a public execution?"

Your screenplay should feel *lean but rich.* Every word should point to something. Every scene should move the plot or deepen the characters. Don't let the weight of history slow you down. Instead, let it *press into the characters,* into their clothes, their fears, their rituals, their silences. Let the historical world be a stage—and let your story burn on it.

Finally, when you finish your first draft, use ChatGPT as your script doctor. Ask, "Which scenes feel slow or out of place?" or "What visual transitions could improve the flow between these two scenes?" You can even say, "Help me rewrite this scene with more tension and fewer words." Screenwriting is rewriting—and having a brainstorming partner who doesn't get tired or precious can make a massive difference.

Because at the end of the day, writing a screenplay from a historical outline is about transformation. You're turning research into rhythm, fact into feeling, silence into cinema. And when you do it right, history doesn't just unfold—it *lives.* One moment, one line, one glance at a time.

Creating Cinematic Moments from Historical Atmosphere

In historical drama, it's not just what happens that matters—it's *how it feels*. You can write the most accurate scene in the world, perfectly plotted and beautifully structured, but if it doesn't feel *lived in*, it won't land. That's where atmosphere steps in. And when used right, atmosphere isn't just background—it becomes the emotional undertow of a moment. It whispers meaning through wind, through candlelight, through the way a curtain lifts in a silent room. Great screenwriting for historical drama depends on turning those atmospheric ingredients into cinematic moments that burn themselves into the memory of the audience.

So what exactly is atmosphere in historical storytelling? It's the sensory experience of the past. It's how the air tastes in a plague-ridden city, how footsteps echo in the marble halls of a crumbling empire, how firelight flickers across the faces of a secret rebellion in a tavern basement. You don't have to explain it—you *show* it. You *feel* it. It's the mood before the words, the tension before the conflict, the emotional weather that shapes everything.

Cinematic moments are born in the space where atmosphere and character collide. That means asking, what is my character feeling—and how can the world reflect or contrast with that feeling in a visual, symbolic way?

Let's say a noblewoman is being forced to marry a man she doesn't love. Instead of starting with dialogue, imagine her walking barefoot across the cold stone floor of a cathedral at dawn. The air is damp. The sun isn't up yet. The stained glass windows are grey, colorless. The silence is so heavy she feels like she might drown in it. That's not just a setting. That's *atmosphere* speaking. That's the world matching her dread, echoing her suffocation.

You can ask ChatGPT to help shape these kinds of moments: "Give me a visual and atmospheric scene that shows a woman preparing for a politically arranged marriage in 18th-century France," or "Describe the mood of a battlefield the night before the final charge in the American Civil War." These scenes don't need to be long. They need to be *felt*.

Atmosphere also gives your historical setting specificity. Instead of a generic "village," give us muddy roads, goats crying in the distance, the smell of burning peat, the sound of a rusty gate blowing in the wind. Instead of a "castle," give us the drip of water through stone, tapestries that stir slightly when a door opens, candlelight quivering in the draft. Use ChatGPT to layer in these details: "What would a winter morning in a 14th-century Polish village sound and smell like?" or "Describe the oppressive mood of a dungeon in Renaissance Spain."

But here's the trick: you don't add detail just for the sake of realism. You add detail to support the *emotion* of the scene.

A rebel hiding in the attic doesn't just hear footsteps below—he hears the boards creak like a heartbeat. A girl watching her brother ride off to war doesn't just see the horses disappear into fog—she sees the fog swallow their faces. These are not neutral details. They're emotionally *charged*—they're part of the cinematic experience.

Music also plays a role in your writing, even if it won't literally appear in your script. The rhythm of your sentences, the choice of imagery, the pauses between actions—all of this creates an emotional tempo. Think of a funeral scene where no one speaks, but the atmosphere does all the work: crows circling above, mourners in black with mud clinging to their boots, a single child standing apart, holding a crumpled ribbon. It's not the dialogue that will be remembered. It's that image. That *feeling*.

You can ask ChatGPT to help generate symbolic visuals based on emotion. Try, "What's a visual metaphor for betrayal in a 19th-century Russian court?" or "Give me an atmospheric image that captures the collapse of hope in a famine-stricken Irish town." These images often say more than an entire paragraph of dialogue.

Lighting is another crucial part of creating atmosphere. Think about the difference between a midday sun and a storm-clouded afternoon. Think of torchlight in a Roman catacomb versus lanterns swaying in the fog outside a Victorian asylum. You're not just lighting the space—you're lighting the *mood*. And every shift in lighting can mirror a shift in power, emotion, or clarity. Ask ChatGPT, "Describe a change in lighting that reflects a character's emotional breakdown in a medieval monastery."

Atmosphere can also be built through sound. A whistle that signals danger. The silence after a gunshot. The chant of protesters rising in the distance. The clatter of armor growing louder in a corridor. Sounds work especially well when paired with tension. The quieter the scene, the more every creak, breath, or drip stands out.

Let your audience feel the past closing in around the character. When someone walks through a devastated village after a battle, let the wind carry ash, let the buildings still smolder, let a single baby cry in the distance. Don't describe the whole war. Show the silence *after* the war. That's atmosphere. That's cinema.

Even nature becomes a participant in a cinematic moment. A crow landing on a gallows. A red sky before a raid. A sudden storm hitting a wedding ceremony. These are not just random events—they become part of the storytelling. Use ChatGPT to help brainstorm: "What kind of natural events could symbolically mirror a power struggle between a king and his advisor in 16th-century Scotland?" or "What would the weather feel like on the night a secret rebellion begins in an Eastern European forest village?"

And the best part? These atmospheric moments don't have to be expensive, sprawling, or filled with extras. They can be intimate. A single candle going out in a church. A door slowly swinging open. A character walking through a childhood home turned into ruins. These moments, built through atmospheric precision, carry enormous weight—and often say more than words ever could.

So when you sit down to write your scenes, ask not just what happens. Ask how it *feels*. What does the world around your character know that they don't? What is the wind saying? What is the light revealing? What does the silence leave behind?

Because when you master atmosphere, your story stops being history on a page.

It becomes a living world.

One breath. One shadow. One flicker of firelight at a time.

Writing a Historical Short Story in One Sitting

The idea of writing an entire historical short story in one sitting might sound like an impossible feat—especially when you're dealing with the demands of period-accurate detail, layered emotion, and narrative structure. But here's the truth: you absolutely can do it. The key isn't to write something perfect. It's to write something *focused*. Something that captures a moment, a voice, or a turning point so vividly that the reader feels like they've stepped straight into the past. If you can write with clarity, emotional precision, and just enough historical texture to create atmosphere, you can build a complete, powerful historical short story in a single creative sprint.

First things first: let go of the idea that you need to cover years of history or explain an entire conflict. A short story doesn't need to teach history—it needs to *feel like it lived in history*. Focus on a single moment in time, a single choice, or a single relationship that plays out in the space of a few pages. The smaller the frame, the more powerful the result. One meal. One letter. One secret. One hour before an execution. These micro-narratives are where historical short stories shine.

Let's say you want to write a story set during the American Revolution. You don't need to recount every battle. Instead, write about a farmer hiding a British soldier in his barn for one night, not knowing whether to help him or hand him over. That story can explore loyalty, fear, and morality—all while never leaving the farm. You can ask ChatGPT, "Help me write a short story set in 1777 where a farmer shelters an enemy soldier and questions his own patriotism." Now you've got a frame—and that's half the battle.

Start your story in motion. No long prologues. No historical summaries. Drop the reader straight into the middle of something that matters. A widow waking up to a knocking at her door in 1863. A child stealing bread during the Great Fire of London. A woman signing a forbidden letter in 1938 Berlin. The reader doesn't need the context up front. They'll learn as they go. And the mystery of the moment will carry them forward.

Use ChatGPT to write your opening lines: "Give me a tense first paragraph for a story about a Jewish mother hiding her daughter during a Nazi raid," or "Write the first few lines of a short story set in an underground printing press during the French Revolution." You're looking for something with emotional grip and immediate stakes.

Once you're inside the story, keep it tight. Two or three characters max. A limited setting. Short stories thrive on constraint. You don't need crowd scenes, sprawling locations, or exposition-heavy dialogue. What you need are *choices*. A character wants something, and something—or someone—is in the way. That's it. A young girl wants to save her family's last cow during a blizzard in 1880s Montana. A prisoner wants to say goodbye to his daughter before execution in 1790s Paris. A cook in an English manor wants to poison her employer after years of abuse. All of these are complete stories if you zoom in on the emotional stakes.

Let your dialogue carry both the weight of history and the personality of your characters. Don't overthink accents or authenticity. Instead, ask, "What does this person need to say—and what are they too afraid to say?" ChatGPT can help you refine this: "Write a tense dialogue between a plantation owner and a runaway slave confronting each other in a storm," or "Create a quiet scene between a mother and son hiding in an attic during a revolution."

Don't get bogged down by period detail. One or two strong atmospheric touches are enough to set the time and place. The clang of a blacksmith's hammer. The flicker of candlelight across a wanted poster. The smell of coal smoke in a tenement hallway. These details paint a world without crowding the story. You can ask ChatGPT, "Describe the atmosphere of a port town in the 1600s during a storm," or "What would a Russian political prisoner's cell look and sound like in 1910?"

Structure your story simply: a compelling beginning, a conflict or discovery in the middle, and a shift or change by the end. Your character doesn't need to win or lose. But something should be different. Even if it's just a change in how they see the world. A girl who's always been afraid now tells her truth. A soldier who's always obeyed now turns away. A man who hated his father finds something in his handwriting that makes him pause. That's resolution—subtle, but resonant.

And when you get to the end, don't explain it. End with an image. A gesture. A line of dialogue. Let it hang. Let it echo. ChatGPT can help you craft this kind of closing: "Give me a final paragraph for a short story where a woman lets go of her son's coat and watches him walk into war," or "Write a closing image for a story about a forgotten grave being discovered by a modern-day archaeologist."

The power of writing a historical short story in one sitting is that it allows you to write *without fear*. You're not outlining a series. You're not writing a novel. You're capturing lightning in a bottle. And yes, it may need editing later. But the bones will be there—the emotion, the moment, the meaning.

So if you're ready, sit down with a strong opening image, a clear emotional arc, and just enough historical weight to ground the world. Ask ChatGPT anything you need to push through the uncertain parts. Keep your setting close, your characters clear, and your ending clean.

And write it. All of it. In one burst.

Because sometimes, the past speaks loudest when it's told in one breath. One night. One unforgettable sitting.

Turning a Historical Novel into a Screenplay

Adapting a historical novel into a screenplay is both an act of compression and transformation. You're not simply rewriting a story for a new format—you're reshaping it for a completely different medium. A novel is internal, detailed, and expansive. A screenplay is visual, external, and driven by rhythm. In a novel, you can spend a page exploring a character's thoughts as they walk through a dusty corridor. In a screenplay, that corridor—and everything it implies—has to be felt in a single image or moment. The emotional depth remains, but the way you reveal it changes completely.

The first step in turning your historical novel into a screenplay is to let go of the idea that every subplot, character, or chapter needs to make it over intact. What you're looking for is the *spine* of the story. That's the emotional through-line—the heartbeat that moves from beginning to end. Strip everything back until you're left with a core premise, a protagonist with a goal, clear stakes, and a journey that can be told in two hours or less. That's your foundation.

Let's say your novel spans ten years, three wars, and multiple generations. The screenplay might only focus on one central relationship across a crucial three-month period. If your novel includes twenty speaking characters, the script might need to merge or cut most of them to keep the story tight. You're not losing the soul of the novel—you're giving it focus. You can ask ChatGPT for help here: "What would be a streamlined two-hour adaptation of a historical novel set during the fall of the Ottoman Empire?" or "Help me identify which characters are essential to adapt from this novel into a feature screenplay."

Next, identify the *cinematic moments* already in your novel—scenes with strong visuals, emotional impact, and natural tension. A duel. A riot. A whispered conversation in a candlelit chapel. A letter burning. These are the moments that translate well to the screen. Mark them in your manuscript, and use them as your screenplay's narrative anchors. You can build the entire script around these visual set pieces and their emotional consequences.

Then, look at what needs to be *shown* instead of *told*. Novels are filled with internal monologues, backstory, exposition, and reflection. In a screenplay, those elements must be translated into action and subtext. If your character in the novel spends five pages mourning a lost love, the screenplay might show them staring at a locket, lighting a candle at a grave, or nearly speaking their name before going quiet. You can ask ChatGPT, "How can I visually express grief without dialogue in a 19th-century French setting?" or "What action might a former slave take in a scene to show he's still haunted by the past without saying a word?"

Dialogue in a screenplay also differs from that in a novel. In fiction, you have room for subtlety and length. In screenwriting, every line must serve a purpose—move the plot, reveal character, or shift emotion. You want dialogue that is sharp, natural, and layered with meaning. If your novel contains poetic monologues or philosophical debates, those might need to be trimmed down into one or two pointed lines that say just enough. Use ChatGPT to refine or rewrite: "Condense this monologue into a short, emotionally charged exchange between two war survivors," or "Rewrite this historical debate scene to work as a tense, two-minute argument in a screenplay."

Now let's talk structure. While a novel might follow a more organic or sprawling structure, a screenplay is tightly organized. Typically, it follows a three-act model: setup, confrontation, and resolution. You'll need a clear inciting incident, midpoint twist, climax, and final beat. Take your novel's plot and map it into a sequence of 30–40 scenes, each serving a clear dramatic function. Ask ChatGPT for help like, "Break my historical novel into a three-act screenplay structure with a turning point every 15–20 pages," or "What's a strong midpoint for a story about a woman hiding Jews in Nazi-occupied Poland?"

You'll also need to consider time compression. In a novel, you can afford to slow the pace. In a screenplay, you have to keep the audience engaged visually and emotionally every few minutes. Scenes must flow into each other, and the story's momentum has to build with each new decision or conflict. If your novel uses time jumps or flashbacks, make sure they're cinematic—easy to follow, and emotionally resonant. ChatGPT can help here: "How can I reframe multiple flashbacks into one powerful visual sequence in a screenplay?" or "What's a visual transition that can signal a 10-year time jump in a historical drama?"

When it comes to setting and costume, remember that you don't need to describe everything. Screenwriters give just enough detail to suggest the world—and let the director, production designer, and costume team take over. Describe what the audience *must* see to understand the scene and the stakes. For example: "INT. ROYAL CHAMBER – NIGHT – Silk banners flutter in the torchlight. Blood stains the marble." You can still evoke your novel's rich historical texture, but do it with tight, impactful language.

And finally, give your screenplay the same emotional core your novel had. A historical film isn't about history—it's about people living through it. Keep your characters complex, your relationships grounded, and your conflicts sharp. The audience won't remember every costume detail—but they will remember the look two characters shared before the sword dropped, or the decision made in silence at a dinner table.

Use ChatGPT as your scene generator, emotional translator, or structure assistant. Ask for help with pacing, visual metaphors, character arcs, or period detail. You might try, "Turn this paragraph of prose into a screenplay scene," or "Write a visual, emotional climax for a story about betrayal in the Russian royal court."

Because adapting a historical novel into a screenplay isn't just a matter of conversion—it's an act of transformation. You're not just retelling the story.

You're reimagining it for light, sound, silence, and image—for the screen, where history breathes in flickering moments, and memory becomes cinema.

Exploring Gender and Identity in Historical Contexts

Writing gender and identity into historical drama means stepping into a world where the rules were often strict, the roles predefined, and the punishments for stepping outside them very real. But it also means uncovering all the ways people resisted, redefined, and reimagined who they were—even when they had to do it in secret. Every historical era carried expectations about what it meant to be a man or a woman—or neither—and those expectations shaped everything from how people dressed and worked to who they loved, feared, or pretended to be. And this is where some of the most powerful, emotionally charged storytelling can happen—right at the intersection between personal truth and cultural restriction.

To explore gender in a historical setting, start by understanding the boundaries. In many time periods, gender roles weren't just social customs—they were law. A woman couldn't inherit land. A man couldn't cry without ridicule. A nonbinary identity might not even have had a name in Western society, though many Indigenous and non-Western cultures embraced gender fluidity in ways European empires tried to erase. So when you write characters in these historical environments, think about the pressure they're under to conform. Then think about what happens when they *can't*.

Imagine a young woman in Victorian England who wants to become a doctor. She might disguise herself as a man, not because she wants to deny her identity, but because it's the only way to practice medicine. That's not just a plot—it's a commentary on gender, ambition, and survival. Or think of a character assigned male at birth who lives as a woman during the American Civil War, and no one knows until years later. These characters aren't anachronisms. They existed. And telling their stories means honoring the real struggles that were often buried by history.

Ask ChatGPT to help you brainstorm based on real constraints. You can say, "What would be the legal and social risks for a woman living as a man in 14th-century Europe?" or "Were there any historical records of gender-nonconforming individuals in Edo-period Japan?" You might be surprised by how much real material is out there, ready to inform your fiction.

The beauty of historical drama is that it allows you to show identity as something that's discovered in conflict. When a character begins to feel tension between who they are and who they're told to be, you don't need to explain everything—they just need to make choices that reveal their truth. A woman cutting her hair. A man refusing to fight. A person who finds joy in both dresses and swords. These aren't just gestures—they're acts of resistance, and they tell us everything we need to know.

Dialogue becomes especially important here. What can be said—and what *can't*? A servant might know her mistress's secret, but never speak it aloud. A soldier might confide in a friend, but in careful, coded language. A mother might pretend not to understand her child's truth, even while protecting them fiercely. These scenes, full of subtext and tension, can be some of the most powerful moments in your story. Use ChatGPT to shape them: "Write a scene between two lovers in a time when their relationship is forbidden, but they never say it out loud," or "Create a dialogue between a transmasc character and their mentor in a medieval guild, where both speak in metaphor."

Symbols can also help you explore gender and identity visually. Clothing, jewelry, hair, posture—these things signal identity even when words are dangerous. A woman passing as a man might carry a token from her past life. A man exploring femininity might keep his reflection hidden from others but practice dancing in secret. These moments don't need to be big. They just need to be honest.

Historical gender norms also create tension between characters. A father who expects his daughter to marry into power. A wife who quietly earns more respect than her husband. A nonbinary character forced into a binary world but slowly carving out space for themselves. The clash between identity and expectation isn't always explosive—it can be slow, sad, defiant, hopeful. Use those emotional textures to guide your story.

Religion, class, and race all interact with gender identity, too. A Black woman in 19th-century America faced different constraints than a white woman in the same position. A highborn lady in ancient China had different expectations than a street performer. A monk might struggle between devotion and desire. These layers of identity don't need to be explained with commentary—they should be *felt* in the character's world, their choices, their consequences.

Ask ChatGPT to help with specific situations: "Describe the internal conflict of a gender-nonconforming character raised in a conservative Muslim household in medieval Persia," or "What societal limitations would a queer nobleman face in 17th-century France, and how might he resist them?" These prompts let you build stories that are both historically grounded and emotionally resonant.

You don't have to use modern language to tell modern truths. You can write about trans, queer, or gender-defiant characters without ever using the word "trans" or "queer." Just show them *being*, struggling, surviving. Let their identity live in action and emotion. The audience will understand—even when the character doesn't have the words yet.

And finally, remember that identity in history wasn't always tragic. There was joy. There was tenderness. There was chosen family, secret weddings, dances in the moonlight, love letters hidden in books. Let your characters experience that too. Don't just show them suffering—show them living, loving, laughing, even if only for a moment. Those moments matter.

Because exploring gender and identity in historical contexts isn't just about revealing oppression—it's about reclaiming agency. It's about telling the stories that history left out, or silenced, or buried in footnotes.

And when you bring those stories to life with honesty, empathy, and imagination, you don't just tell the truth.

You give the past a voice it was never allowed to use.

Injecting Mystery, Romance, and Suspense into History

Historical drama can be rich with emotion, conflict, and atmosphere—but if you really want to keep your audience turning pages or glued to the screen, blending in elements of mystery, romance, and suspense can supercharge the entire experience. These genres aren't distractions from the historical setting—they're tools that pull the past into sharper focus. They heighten stakes, deepen character, and make the emotional tension sing. When done right, mystery, romance, and suspense aren't additions—they become the heart of the story.

Let's start with mystery. History is already full of unknowns—lost letters, vanished people, missing records, strange alliances, unexplained deaths. It only takes one gap in the historical record to open the door for fiction to step in and ask, *What if?* Maybe a nobleman's sudden death wasn't from illness but poison. Maybe a royal decree was forged. Maybe a spy was hidden in plain sight for years. You don't have to write a murder mystery to add a layer of intrigue—just create a question at the center of your story that your protagonist must slowly uncover.

Ask ChatGPT to help you build these: "Give me a historical mystery setup involving a missing priest in 1600s Spain," or "What secret could a nurse uncover in a WWI hospital that would put her life at risk?" These mysteries work especially well in historical settings because secrecy was often a matter of life or death. There were no internet leaks, no DNA tests—just rumours, letters, stolen glances, and buried truths.

Romance, on the other hand, can be the beating heart of your historical drama. The rules of love in the past were harsh and complicated—marriages arranged for power, same-sex relationships criminalized, lovers separated by class, race, religion, or war. This makes romance more than just emotional—it's revolutionary. A stolen kiss in public could mean disgrace. A love letter might have to be encoded. A couple might only meet once every season. The stakes are already high because the world is against them.

What makes historical romance powerful is that it often lives in the shadows. The yearning, the secrecy, the quiet courage. These aren't modern relationships—they're shaped by context, and the beauty comes from the limits. You can ask ChatGPT, "Create a romantic subplot between a soldier and a pacifist nurse during the Crimean War," or "Write a tension-filled scene between a samurai and the daughter of his enemy." The idea isn't to force love into the story—it's to let love *complicate* the story.

Now add suspense. Not every suspenseful story needs a chase or an assassin in the bushes. Historical suspense can come from knowing that the character is one wrong move away from destruction. A revolutionary hiding in the king's court. A child keeping a forbidden book under their mattress. A woman giving birth alone in a war-torn village while soldiers search nearby homes. These scenes burn slowly but carry immense emotional charge. The audience doesn't know when the explosion will come—but they feel it building.

Use ChatGPT to help brainstorm: "What's a suspenseful sequence where a letter must be delivered through enemy lines during the American Civil War?" or "Give me a suspenseful setup where a servant overhears a plot against the queen in Renaissance England." These ideas give your story forward momentum—something is always on the verge of being discovered, lost, or destroyed.

The real magic happens when you *combine* these elements. A mysterious death leads to an unlikely alliance between two characters from different social classes. As they uncover secrets together, they begin to fall in love. But the closer they get to the truth—and to each other—the more dangerous their world becomes. Suddenly, your story is layered, emotionally rich, and utterly addictive.

Let's say you're writing about a woman accused of witchcraft in colonial Massachusetts. The mystery could be: who accused her—and why? The romance: a forbidden relationship with someone in a position of power. The suspense: a trial where the evidence is manipulated, and the outcome could be death. In a few pages, you've got emotional investment, plot twists, and historical grounding all working together.

What's critical when blending genres in historical drama is keeping everything *rooted in the world.* Don't let the mystery, romance, or suspense feel modern or transplanted. Let the limitations of the era heighten everything. The lack of communication technology. The rigid social roles. The deeply held superstitions and laws. These are not obstacles to storytelling—they're what make your story *historical.* A romantic gesture that would be simple today becomes an act of rebellion. A missing document becomes a national scandal. A single witness becomes the difference between life and death.

Atmosphere helps enormously. Let the fog obscure not just the street, but the truth. Let a stolen moment between lovers happen in a candlelit hallway during a masquerade. Let a conversation take place in whispers over a poisoned goblet. These visual, emotional layers are what make your story cinematic, immersive, unforgettable.

Use ChatGPT to explore those sensory elements: "Describe a suspenseful dinner party scene where everyone suspects each other but no one says it," or "Create a romantic moment between two characters separated by a locked door during a plague quarantine."

Ultimately, blending mystery, romance, and suspense into historical drama isn't about adding drama for drama's sake—it's about exposing the *hidden tensions* that already lived in the past. The secrets people took to their graves. The lovers history forgot. The choices that shaped destinies in the shadows. These aren't distractions from history. They *are* history—just told through the lens of emotion, risk, and human longing.

So lean into the secrets. Let the letters go unread, the touches go unseen, the motives go unclear—until they don't.

And when they come together in one final moment, one final truth, let the weight of history come crashing down in silence, fire, or a single whispered name.

That's when your story will stop being a re-enactment.

And start being unforgettable.

Reimagining Famous Figures with a Fresh Lens

When you write historical drama, it's tempting to steer clear of the well-known names. Why compete with centuries of biographies, movies, and documentaries? But the truth is, famous historical figures are some of the richest, most complex characters you'll ever find—because they're not just icons. They're *people*, and the stories we've been told about them are often just one version, one layer, one sliver of who they really were. Reimagining a famous figure with a fresh lens doesn't mean changing history—it means peeling it back to reveal something deeper, something unexpected, something entirely human.

The key is to begin with a question: *What haven't we seen before?* What angle has been overlooked, buried, or ignored? Maybe it's political—reframing Winston Churchill not as a war hero but as a flawed empire-builder. Maybe it's emotional—imagining Joan of Arc not as a fearless saint, but as a terrified teenager holding it together by faith alone. Maybe it's intimate—telling the story of Marie Antoinette through the eyes of her maid, or of Abraham Lincoln as seen through the lens of grief rather than power.

History tends to compress people into symbols. Your job as a storyteller is to *unpack* those symbols. You don't need to rewrite what happened—you just need to add emotional truth to the known facts. If someone was a ruler, show the weight of the crown. If someone was a revolutionary, show the doubt before the battle. If someone was a genius, show the loneliness of never being understood.

Start by choosing the lens. Is it psychological? Are you trying to understand the trauma, guilt, or desire that drove this person's choices? Is it relational? Are you focusing on a forgotten friendship, a secret love, a rivalry that shaped them? Is it political? Are you reframing the impact of their decisions from the perspective of those who suffered under them—or were saved by them? Once you know your lens, you know where to look.

Ask ChatGPT to help you reframe the perspective: "What would the story of Napoleon look like through the eyes of one of his exiled soldiers?" or "Help me write a version of Cleopatra told through the emotional lens of her final hours." You're not creating a historical replica—you're creating an emotional *truth* rooted in history.

Sometimes the key is focusing on a *specific moment* instead of the whole life. Don't try to summarize Alexander the Great. Write about the night before his final battle, or the moment he realizes his empire is too vast to hold. Don't retell the life of Queen Elizabeth I—tell the story of the day she chose not to marry. These narrow windows let you explore character in depth without getting overwhelmed by the epic scope.

You can also reimagine famous figures by placing them in new emotional or cultural contexts. What if you told the story of Leonardo da Vinci through the lens of queerness and secrecy? What if you showed Genghis Khan not through conquests, but through fatherhood? What if you explored Emily Dickinson's poetry as a coded map of her mental world rather than just a literary achievement?

Another powerful technique is to contrast public image with private truth. Show the dissonance between who the world thought they were and who they believed themselves to be. Let Julius Caesar weep in private. Let Florence Nightingale rage against the patriarchy that silenced her data. Let Frederick Douglass struggle with survivor's guilt. These contradictions are what make characters compelling—and believable.

Ask ChatGPT, "What lesser-known events in Frida Kahlo's life could anchor a dramatic short film?" or "What personal regrets might Martin Luther King Jr. have wrestled with privately during the Civil Rights Movement?" These questions generate narrative gold.

You can also shift the spotlight entirely. Tell the story of the famous figure through someone who knew them—a child, a servant, a political opponent, a forgotten lover. This outside perspective allows you to show the character in action rather than explanation. It also lets you create contrast: what they said versus what they did, what they promised versus what they left behind. ChatGPT can help you map these relationships: "Who were the people closest to Pablo Picasso during his blue period?" or "What servant might have worked for Catherine the Great, and what could they have seen that history ignored?"

Historical records are often silent on emotion, silence, vulnerability. That's where fiction steps in. When you reimagine a famous figure, you're not falsifying history—you're *humanizing* it. You're giving shape to the inner life behind the public face. And that's the fresh lens readers crave: not a repeat of what they already know, but a revelation of what they've never been told.

Of course, this comes with responsibility. Do your research. Know the facts well enough to bend them with care. If your story contradicts the historical record, make sure it does so with purpose—not just for shock value or dramatic effect, but to say something meaningful about the time, the character, or the world we live in now. Historical drama is always a conversation between the past and the present. Make that conversation count.

And finally, let your reimagining feel alive. Don't treat the historical figure like a relic. Treat them like a character with breath in their lungs and mud on their boots. Let them laugh, fail, dream, scheme, break, and rebuild. Let them be more than a statue or a painting.

Because when you give new depth to an old name, when you give voice to what history kept quiet, you don't just reimagine the figure.

You reawaken the story.

And that, more than any monument or date, is what keeps history alive.

Building a Fictional Family Tree across Generations

When you write historical drama, especially in novel form or as an epic screenplay, building a fictional family tree across generations can transform your narrative from a single perspective into a rich, layered tapestry of inheritance, trauma, tradition, rebellion, and love. It allows you to show how history doesn't just happen *to* people—it flows *through* them. Names repeat. Secrets echo. Sins return dressed as legacies. And over time, each generation either repeats the mistakes of the past or claws their way toward something better. That's where the true drama lies—in the passage of time written not on the clock, but in the bloodline.

Start with the structure. How many generations will your story span? Two? Four? Ten? You can write a tight dual-timeline story between grandmother and granddaughter, or build a sweeping narrative that moves from the 1600s to the 1960s. The key is choosing anchor points—pivotal events that shape the family across time. A war. A betrayal. An act of love or cruelty that casts a shadow. Use ChatGPT to map this out quickly: "Help me create a four-generation family line starting with a 17th-century Italian widow who becomes a healer," or "Create a historical family tree that begins with a freed slave in 1865 and ends with a civil rights lawyer in 1965."

Each generation should carry something. It might be literal—like a ring, a deed, a letter—or it might be emotional, like guilt, pride, or fear. Think of it as passing a torch—or sometimes, a burden. A revolutionary father might leave behind a cause. A broken mother might pass down silence. A merchant might leave wealth, but not wisdom. These patterns are what connect the generations—not just biologically, but thematically.

Names matter, too. In many historical cultures, children were named after parents or grandparents. The repetition of names can be symbolic—a reminder that history is always circling back. You can also break tradition deliberately: a character who chooses *not* to pass on a name is saying something powerful about change. ChatGPT can help you brainstorm: "What naming traditions were used in Irish families in the 1800s?" or "Suggest symbolic names for a fictional Jewish family spanning five generations."

Each generation should also reflect the era they live in. That means understanding the political, cultural, and social landscape of their time. A woman born in 1850 will face different expectations than her granddaughter in 1920. A son born into a family of aristocrats in the early 1800s might find himself stripped of status by the next century. Let the outside world shape the inside of the family. Ask ChatGPT, "What challenges would a second-generation immigrant family face in 1920s New York?" or "How might a royal family change between the fall of the Austro-Hungarian Empire and the rise of fascism?"

Conflict between generations is often where the most compelling scenes come from. A daughter who wants to join a cause her father fought to avoid. A grandfather who demands obedience while hiding a youthful rebellion of his own. A son raised in wealth who's ashamed of the power it cost his ancestors to build. These conflicts create emotional heat—and they also give you a reason to jump timelines or reveal old secrets.

Family secrets are fuel. A character might uncover a letter, a will, a confession, or a grave. That discovery lets you open a window into the past while propelling the story in the present. Use this to your advantage. One generation hides something. Another one finds it. The emotional ripple travels across decades. Ask ChatGPT, "Give me a plot where a modern-day character uncovers a secret about their ancestor's betrayal during World War II," or "Suggest a way to reveal a hidden identity in a three-generation Cuban-American family."

Don't forget the quieter threads—the rituals, foods, sayings, gestures, and heirlooms that survive across time. A lullaby sung in multiple centuries. A dish prepared only on one holiday. A superstition kept alive even after the meaning is forgotten. These small details humanize your world and give emotional texture to your family tree. You can prompt ChatGPT: "Describe three generational rituals a fictional Mexican family might pass down from the 1800s to today," or "What could be a meaningful object passed from mother to daughter in a Japanese family for 150 years?"

When building your family tree, sketch it out visually. You don't have to write every branch in detail, but mapping it gives you structure. You can create a timeline, list of names, or even a family crest that ties everyone together. Ask ChatGPT to help draw up a simple multi-generational family tree based on your story idea. Then start filling it with moments—births, deaths, migrations, marriages, betrayals, reunions. Let the tree feel alive.

Remember, the generational aspect isn't just about adding backstory—it's about showing the reader that time is not a straight line. That who we are is shaped by who came before us. That a choice made in a single moment can echo for a century. Maybe a man is haunted by something he doesn't even know happened to his great-grandfather. Maybe a child carries the courage of her ancestor without realizing where it came from.

That's the beauty of a generational story—it's not just about characters, but about *inheritance*. Not in terms of money or property, but of identity, belief, pain, hope, and silence.

So build your family not just across time—but across emotion. Let them fight, love, betray, forgive, disappear, and return. Let them repeat history—and sometimes, defy it.

Because when you build a fictional family tree with depth, you're not just writing history.

You're writing how history *lives on*. One name. One scar. One memory at a time.

Handling Multinational Historical Settings

Writing historical drama that spans multiple nations is like conducting an orchestra where each instrument has its own rhythm, voice, and emotional temperature. Every country in your narrative brings its own language, customs, values, conflicts, and political tensions. And if you're not careful, your story can quickly collapse under the weight of too many timelines, accents, and events. But if you approach it with clarity and purpose, multinational historical settings become your secret weapon—a way to show the global ripples of personal and political choices, to dramatize the clash of empires and ideologies, and to follow characters across cultural fault lines that history has carved into the earth.

The first step in managing a multinational setting is to decide *why* the story spans borders. Are you showing the fallout of a single event across continents? Following a family that migrates over time? Weaving together multiple characters who will eventually collide? The why informs the structure. For example, if you're writing about World War I, you might have one thread in France, one in the Ottoman Empire, and another in Russia—each shaped by the same war but told through vastly different lenses. Ask ChatGPT to help build these perspectives: "What three types of characters in different countries could be connected by the events of World War I?"

Multinational historical stories work best when the reader or viewer can emotionally *track* each location. That means giving each setting a distinct tone, atmosphere, and set of stakes. A snowbound village in Finland should feel *cold*—not just physically but emotionally: isolated, haunting, restrained. Meanwhile, a revolutionary café in Havana should buzz with heat, smoke, and risk. You're not just changing place—you're changing the emotional texture of the world. Ask ChatGPT for help evoking these: "Describe the mood of a crumbling French castle in 1789 versus a crowded street in Delhi during British rule."

Language is another challenge in multinational stories—but it can also be a gift. Characters who speak different languages can misunderstand each other, lie more easily, or form bonds without words. Let language be both a barrier and a bridge. A character translating a letter might choose to soften its meaning—or twist it. A multilingual character might move between worlds, hiding parts of themselves depending on what language they're speaking. Use ChatGPT to help shape authentic multilingual exchanges: "Write a scene where a Spanish soldier and a Filipino revolutionary attempt to negotiate without fully understanding each other's language."

History is never neutral, and different countries remember the same events in radically different ways. That's where drama thrives. The British view of the Boer War is not the same as the Afrikaner view. The American narrative of Vietnam is not the same as the Vietnamese perspective. Use these contrasts. Let characters argue history. Let them clash over what "freedom," "loyalty," or "honor" means. These aren't just conflicts—they're windows into culture. Ask ChatGPT to help craft these debates: "Write a conversation between a French colonial officer and an Algerian rebel about the meaning of civilization."

You can also play with structure. Maybe your story is told in parallel timelines across countries, gradually revealing how characters are connected. Maybe it hops locations like a political thriller. Or maybe it starts in one nation and expands outward as the consequences of a single choice ripple through the globe. Think of stories like *The English Patient*, *Cloud Atlas*, or *Babel*—they thrive on multinational structure because their emotional arcs connect the dots. If you're unsure how to structure it, ask ChatGPT, "What's a good screenplay structure for a historical story spanning Germany, Egypt, and Brazil from 1930 to 1950?"

Use travel and communication as narrative pressure points. In the past, information moved slowly. A telegram delayed could change history. A letter intercepted could save a life—or destroy it. A ship lost at sea might carry everything a character needs. Use these gaps in global connection as suspense tools. Ask ChatGPT for plot ideas like, "How could a letter smuggled across WWI front lines create suspense in three connected storylines set in France, Turkey, and Egypt?"

Characters moving between countries—immigrants, refugees, diplomats, soldiers, traders—should feel the weight of cultural transition. One set of rules applies in one land. In another, everything changes. A woman respected as a healer in her homeland might be persecuted as a witch in another. A nobleman might become a beggar. A servant might find unexpected freedom. These shifts create internal and external drama that deepen your characters. Prompt ChatGPT with: "Describe the emotional experience of a Chinese scholar traveling to Victorian London in 1875," or "What challenges would a Jewish child face fleeing Nazi Germany and arriving in neutral Sweden in 1941?"

And don't forget *symbols* and *rituals*. These vary across borders and can serve as anchors to mark transitions. A prayer. A piece of clothing. A dish prepared in exile. These small, recurring elements can carry emotional weight and bind together global storylines. They help keep your characters grounded, even as the world shifts beneath their feet.

The challenge of a multinational historical drama is also what makes it exhilarating: you're writing across empires, time zones, and ideologies. You're showing that history isn't a single story—it's a web of interconnected lives, often far apart in space but close in spirit. You're inviting readers to see not just how people lived, but how people *struggled to live* when caught between two or more worlds.

So let the borders be real. Let the languages clash. Let the distances feel enormous. Then let your characters bridge them with love, fear, rebellion, survival, silence, and hope.

Because when you handle multinational historical settings with care and imagination, you're not just writing about the past.

You're writing about how far people will go to find truth in a divided world—and how far we still carry those journeys today.

Finding Emotion in the Midst of Historical Catastrophe

Catastrophe is often the backbone of historical drama—wars, plagues, genocides, invasions, revolutions. These are the events that shape timelines and topple empires. But if you focus only on the scale of disaster, you risk losing the soul of the story. What makes historical catastrophe compelling isn't the numbers. It's the individuals. The ones who live, the ones who don't, the ones who love in secret, break in silence, or fight when no one's watching. In the middle of fire, rubble, and grief, your job as a storyteller is to find *emotion*—to create intimacy inside the chaos.

The audience doesn't remember body counts—they remember a child crying in an empty street. They remember the old man who locks the door one last time. The woman who keeps stirring the soup even though she knows no one's coming home. It's these human-scale moments that make catastrophe real. And in historical storytelling, the smaller the moment, the more powerful the impact.

Start by grounding your story in one character. One person whose world is unraveling. This character doesn't have to be a soldier, a leader, or a revolutionary. They can be a tailor, a baker, a teacher, a servant. The catastrophe—whether it's a war or a fire or a famine—can unfold around them while their personal life is thrown into crisis. Use ChatGPT to help you build this perspective: "Give me a character sketch of a midwife during the fall of Berlin," or "Create a story idea centered around a teenage farmer during the Dust Bowl."

Now think about what they want *in spite of* the disaster. Do they want to find their family? Finish one last letter? Save one more life? Sometimes the strongest emotional arc is a small, quiet one. Not surviving the whole war—but walking one person to safety. Not ending oppression—but burying a child with dignity. These moments don't try to explain history. They make it *felt*.

Let your characters process catastrophe emotionally, not just physically. Show the shock, the denial, the numbness. But don't rush them to heroism. Sometimes the most honest choice is to have your character freeze when they should run. Cry when they should stay silent. Lie to survive. That's not weakness—that's reality. Ask ChatGPT, "Describe the emotional reaction of a man who returns to his home after a bombing to find only rubble," or "Write a short scene where a girl hides with her brother in the woods after their village is burned."

Let environment echo emotion. If a city is burning, focus on the heat on the skin. If the plague has emptied the streets, focus on the silence, the sound of wind against boarded windows. These details speak louder than exposition. You don't need to explain what happened—just show what's left behind. A broken toy. A letter no one will read. A door still swinging open. Ask ChatGPT for imagery like, "What would a synagogue in Kraków look like days after a Nazi raid?" or "Describe the atmosphere in a coastal town a week after a tsunami in 1755."

In scenes of catastrophe, time stretches and contracts. One second might last a page. Or you might skip weeks in a single sentence. Use pacing to reflect trauma. Slow down to show disorientation. Speed up to create panic. Let the rhythm of the scene match the emotion. You can ask ChatGPT, "How do I write a slow, emotional scene where a mother washes her child's body during a cholera outbreak?" or "Write a breathless, high-stakes sequence where villagers flee a volcanic eruption in the 1600s."

Even in disaster, let there be connection. Two strangers clasping hands. A final act of kindness. A joke whispered in the dark. These human moments are how people endure—and how audiences remember. You don't need a happy ending. But you do need an emotional heartbeat. Someone the audience roots for. Someone who doesn't just witness history, but feels it to their core.

Flashbacks can also help when writing about catastrophe. Show what life was like *before*. A dinner table. A wedding. A song. These glimpses into the past give the present more weight. They remind us what was lost. Ask ChatGPT, "Write a memory sequence for a woman who used to dance at the opera before the city was invaded," or "Create a moment where a soldier remembers his brother teaching him to fish, just before going into battle."

Symbols help anchor emotion. A necklace that survives a fire. A piece of clothing passed from one character to another. A photograph that keeps getting folded and unfolded. These objects carry memory and emotion through the chaos. They help tell the story without dialogue. You can ask ChatGPT, "What symbolic item could a refugee mother carry with her from Spain during the Civil War?" or "What object could represent hope to a prisoner in a Siberian gulag?"

And let your characters change. Catastrophe reshapes people. Someone who was brave becomes broken. Someone who was selfish becomes selfless. Someone who was forgotten becomes a witness. These arcs give your story emotional depth. You don't need to tie every thread neatly—but show transformation, however subtle. Let the experience mark your characters physically or emotionally—whether they make it through or not.

Lastly, let there be silence. Don't over-explain what the audience can feel. Don't fill every pause with dialogue. In the aftermath of historical tragedy, sometimes the most powerful thing is a character standing alone, looking at what's gone, unable to speak.

Because in the midst of historical catastrophe, what matters most isn't the scale of the destruction.

It's the single heart still beating in the rubble.

That's the story worth telling.

How to Make Readers Feel the Cost of Change

Change is at the heart of historical drama. Revolutions rise, empires fall, industries roar to life, beliefs crumble, and borders are redrawn. These shifts are the engines of plot—but if you want your story to *move* people, you can't just show change. You have to make them *feel the cost of it.* You have to write so that the reader doesn't just understand what's different, but senses, in their bones, what it took to get there—what was lost, broken, burned, or left behind in the name of progress, freedom, or survival.

Historical change is never clean. It doesn't arrive in neat packages. It comes through blood, betrayal, silence, abandonment, risk, and sacrifice. So when you're writing about it, you don't just track events. You track *impact.* What does this change mean for one family? One marriage? One friendship? What tradition is shattered? What home is leveled? What dream is buried because the world no longer has room for it?

Start small. Think of a character who's just lost something they didn't realize they were about to lose. Maybe it's the right to speak their language. Maybe it's their job, handed to someone half their age and from a different class. Maybe it's the meaning of their uniform. These aren't just practical losses—they're identity-shaking. Use ChatGPT to help find moments like these: "What would a blacksmith lose when industrial machinery replaces his trade in 19th-century England?" or "Describe the emotional toll on a samurai watching Japan westernize."

Change also hurts when it creates *division.* One sibling joins a rebellion, the other enlists with the empire. One friend adapts to the new rules, the other resists. One parent clings to the old religion, the child leaves it behind. These emotional ruptures are where your story breathes. Readers don't just want to see change—they want to watch someone *choose* it, or *refuse* it, and live with the consequences. Ask ChatGPT for scene ideas like, "Write a dialogue between two sisters during the Russian Revolution, one who joins the Bolsheviks and one who doesn't," or "Give me a scene where a plantation owner and his son argue over abolition."

To make the cost of change land, *slow it down.* Show the rituals breaking. The silence after the festival isn't held. The closing of a family shop. The wedding that doesn't happen because two people are now on opposite sides of a border. Let your characters experience the absence. Don't just tell the reader something is gone—let them sit in the space where it used to be. Ask ChatGPT, "How might a Jewish tailor experience the transition into Nazi-occupied territory?" or "What small daily routines would disappear for a woman after the fall of the Qing Dynasty?"

Memory is another powerful tool. Flashbacks, dreams, or even hallucinations can show us what the world *used* to be, so that the reader feels the contrast with the present. These aren't there to give exposition—they're there to stir loss. A character might recall their mother singing a banned song, or a holiday that no longer exists. Even a simple image—candlelight on a child's face, a garden no longer tended—can carry the full emotional weight of what change has taken. Use prompts like, "Give me a memory scene for a man who used to be a prince before his kingdom was overthrown," or "Describe a recurring dream of a refugee about the home they can't return to."

Let your characters feel ambivalence. Change doesn't always feel like victory, even when it's necessary. The abolitionist who loses their livelihood. The general who wins the war but loses their child. The widow whose freedom arrives just as her family dissolves. These contradictions are the soul of historical drama—they're what keep your story from becoming simplistic. When your characters don't know how to feel, that's when the reader feels the most.

Symbols can make change visible. A flag lowered. A dress no longer worn. A language stopped mid-sentence. An heirloom pawned. A tradition laughed at by the next generation. Let these physical markers of change enter and exit your story at the right moments. You can ask ChatGPT, "What symbolic objects could represent the loss of tradition in a Greek family during World War II?" or "What might a freed slave carry that reminds them of bondage, even in freedom?"

Even hopeful change has a cost. A woman winning the right to vote may lose the protection of her social class. A child learning a new language may feel like they're betraying their grandparents. Change often feels like letting go before it feels like arriving. Capture that ache. Let it be messy, tender, unresolved. That's where your readers find themselves.

If your story moves across time, show how later generations *inherit* the cost of change. A modern descendant who finds letters, heirlooms, scars they can't quite explain. They carry the story, even if they don't know it. That's how history works—it never really ends. It ripples.

To write historical change in a way that truly matters, you don't need to explain the politics or outline the reforms. You need to show a mother burning old clothes in a barrel. A lover writing a letter they never send. A man staring at a machine that just made his hands obsolete. That's what the reader remembers.

Because change in history isn't just the beginning of something new. It's always the end of something else.

And when you write the *cost* of that end—clearly, quietly, truthfully—your story becomes not just a record of what happened...

It becomes a testimony to what was paid.

Writing for Modern Audiences with Historical Respect

When writing historical drama, you're always caught in a delicate balancing act. On one side, you want to immerse your audience in the world of the past—its culture, customs, values, and voices. On the other, you're writing for modern readers or viewers whose expectations, ethics, and sensitivities are shaped by the world we live in now. This creates tension, and that tension is creative fuel. But it also demands care. Because your job isn't just to retell history. It's to *interpret* it in a way that resonates today without flattening, distorting, or romanticizing what really happened.

Respecting history doesn't mean being rigid. It means being *conscious*. It means knowing when you're using imagination to fill in the blanks—and when you're erasing uncomfortable truths to make a story more convenient or palatable. Modern audiences can smell the difference. They want authenticity, but they also want clarity of purpose. They want to feel like the past is alive and real—but not like it's being used as an excuse for outdated thinking or stereotypes.

The first step is to understand the *real world* of your story's time period. That means more than costumes and dates. It means knowing how power worked—who had it, who didn't, and how that shaped every aspect of daily life. You don't need to lecture your audience, but you do need to *know your world* deeply enough that your characters aren't behaving like modern people in historical clothing. Use ChatGPT to help you explore this: "What were the social limitations on a lower-class woman in 1820s Paris?" or "How would a Chinese immigrant be treated in California during the 1880s?"

Modern readers want emotional truth—but they also crave moral complexity. Don't be afraid to show flawed characters. Just don't present injustice without context. If your story includes slavery, colonialism, misogyny, or systemic violence, acknowledge it clearly. You can still tell stories about people who were complicit in injustice—just don't sanitize or glamorize it. Let your characters wrestle with their choices. Let the consequences be real. You don't have to solve history—but you shouldn't ignore it either.

One way to bridge the past and present is through *intimacy*. Show what a law or war or belief system did to a single person. How it bent their life, hardened their heart, or broke their spirit. When a character's pain feels real, readers connect—even across centuries. Don't tell us slavery was cruel. Show us the man burying his wife in a shallow grave because she wasn't treated. Don't tell us women had no power. Show us the young girl burning her own poems because no one would ever read them. Those are the scenes that carry historical weight.

Language is another big challenge. You want to sound of the time, but you also want to stay accessible. You don't have to write in exact dialects or replicate archaic grammar—but you do want to avoid modern slang, phrasing, and attitudes that would break the illusion. Ask ChatGPT to help you strike that balance: "Write a conversation between two Victorian women about inheritance that sounds authentic but is still readable," or "Give me a historically grounded way for a 15th-century knight to express fear without using modern words."

Don't be afraid to let modern *themes* echo through your historical story—but do it through character and situation, not speeches. You can write about freedom, gender roles, racism, or justice—but let those ideas rise organically from the story. A character doesn't need to be woke by today's standards. They just need to *feel*—to doubt, to question, to break a rule even if they don't have the words for why. That's how you give modern audiences something to hold onto without turning your historical drama into a lecture or a fantasy.

One of the most powerful ways to respect history is by showing *silenced voices*. So much of recorded history was written by the winners, the rulers, the rich. Your job as a storyteller is to bring in those who were pushed aside—the servants, the soldiers, the women, the children, the colonized, the persecuted, the unheard. You're not rewriting history—you're completing it. Ask ChatGPT, "Help me write a story from the perspective of a palace cook during the fall of the Romanovs," or "What might a freedwoman in 1870s Georgia want to say but not be allowed to?"

It's also okay to subvert expectations—gently. If your audience thinks they know a time period, surprise them. Show the complexity. The contradictions. The beauty in unlikely places and the ugliness in those history called heroes. Don't flatten your world into black and white. Show the grays. Show the moments that challenge modern assumptions. Show the past as a mirror—not just a museum.

You can also use structure to connect with modern audiences. Jump timelines. Use dual narratives. Open with a modern discovery of a historical secret. Frame a story within a story. These techniques can help modern readers find their way into unfamiliar eras. Ask ChatGPT, "Give me a framing device for a novel where a modern scholar uncovers letters from a 17th-century nun," or "Suggest a dual-timeline structure for a story set in colonial India and modern-day London."

Finally, remember that historical respect isn't about accuracy alone—it's about *intention*. Write with empathy. Write with curiosity. Write with a willingness to be surprised. The past wasn't perfect, but it was real. When you treat it with care, you give your audience something richer than facts. You give them connection. You let them feel that people then were not so different from people now—struggling, surviving, loving, failing, hoping.

So write the past truthfully. Write it passionately. Write it with an open mind and a steady hand.

Because when you write historical drama for modern audiences with respect, you're not just showing where we've been.

You're showing why it still matters.

Letting the Past Speak to the Present

One of the most profound powers of historical drama is its ability to hold up a mirror—not just to the past, but to *right now*. When you write about ancient empires, old revolutions, or vanished traditions, you're never just writing about what happened. You're writing about what still echoes. The fears we haven't buried. The injustices we haven't corrected. The hopes we still carry. Letting the past speak to the present doesn't mean hammering your reader over the head with modern commentary. It means weaving subtle threads between then and now—letting them feel that even across centuries, human experience doesn't change as much as we think.

To do this well, you start with theme. Ask yourself: What is this story *really* about underneath the corsets, the battles, the candles and quills? Is it about freedom? Control? Belief? Belonging? The moment you identify the emotional and philosophical backbone of your story, you can begin to draw connections. A story set during the Spanish Inquisition may resonate with modern debates about censorship and extremism. A drama about a 19th-century woman fighting to be educated may echo in today's conversations about gender equity and access. Let those parallels simmer quietly in the background of your narrative.

Don't force them. Let them breathe.

One powerful way to let the past speak is to write contradictions into your characters—people struggling with ideas ahead of their time, or people clinging to systems that no longer serve them. These characters become bridges. A slave who dreams of freedom despite never having seen it. A noble who defends tradition but can no longer justify its cruelty. These inner conflicts reflect the ones we still carry in the modern world—how we evolve, what we resist, what we fear losing.

Ask ChatGPT to help you explore these bridges: "Create a character in 1600s Florence who secretly questions the Catholic Church," or "Write a scene between two lovers in 1910 Istanbul whose relationship is destroyed by political ideologies." These moments may be locked in time, but the emotion behind them is timeless.

You can also use visual and symbolic storytelling to create resonance. A flag raised in defiance. A forbidden book passed hand to hand. A wedding halted by protest. These images transcend their historical setting. A modern viewer or reader will understand their power intuitively—even if the context is unfamiliar. Ask ChatGPT, "What's a visual symbol of resistance in 18th-century Haiti that would still resonate today?" or "Describe a scene in ancient Persia that would mirror modern struggles with government surveillance."

Another technique is to let your characters speak words that ring with present-day meaning—not because you use modern language, but because the truth is universal. When a character says, "This land belonged to my people before the walls were built," or "I cannot serve a country that does not see me," those lines don't belong to just one era. They belong to all of them.

Letting the past speak to the present also means knowing where not to explain. Trust the reader. Trust that they'll feel it when a woman hides her identity to survive. When a man sacrifices truth for loyalty. When a child watches their world change and doesn't understand why. You don't need to draw a neon arrow from 1745 to 2025. You just need to write the moment with clarity and compassion.

Dual timelines can be helpful here, but they're not required. You can frame your story through a modern discovery of a historical letter, a hidden artifact, a family secret. These devices give your modern reader a touchpoint—and give your historical world a second voice. A modern scholar might not understand what they've found. A descendant might feel shame, pride, or confusion. Let the modern and historical worlds exist in conversation, even if they never touch.

Sometimes, letting the past speak means showing what hasn't changed—and sometimes, what *has*. Maybe your story ends with a glimpse of the future your characters never got to see. A woman who never votes, but whose great-granddaughter becomes a senator. A man imprisoned for who he loves, while his diary is read aloud at a pride march a century later. These moments don't need to be long. They just need to close the loop between time and meaning.

Music, objects, rituals—all of these can connect timelines too. A song sung in different centuries. A recipe passed down. A tattoo that appears in two storylines with different meanings. These are the threads that hold historical drama together, and let your audience feel that the past isn't behind us—it's *with* us.

And finally, be honest. Don't try to tidy history. Let the past be messy, painful, beautiful, unfinished. Your audience doesn't need heroes—they need *truth*. They need to see themselves reflected in people who lived long ago and realize: we're still fighting the same fights. Still dreaming the same dreams. Still building, breaking, loving, resisting.

Because when you let the past speak—not with speeches, but with story—you do more than teach history.

You remind us that we're standing on the shoulders of everyone who came before.

And maybe, just maybe, we're not so different after all.

From Outline to Final Draft in a Single Day

It might sound impossible, even reckless: taking a historical drama from rough outline to finished draft in just one day. But with focus, intention, and the right strategy, you can absolutely pull it off—especially with the help of ChatGPT as your tireless writing partner. The goal here isn't to create a perfect, polished manuscript. It's to write a *complete, emotionally cohesive, and structurally sound* first draft that captures your story's spirit and flow. You'll revise later. For now, it's about momentum, clarity, and making the past come alive on the page with power and urgency.

The first thing you need is your *starting outline*. Whether you've already mapped your chapters or you're just sitting on a few key historical beats and character arcs, now's the time to flesh it out just enough to serve as your blueprint. You don't want an exhaustive breakdown. You want 10 to 20 clear, emotionally charged scenes that move the story forward—from inciting incident to climax to resolution. These aren't just plot points—they're *moments of decision, tension, or transformation.*

Use ChatGPT to help expand your basic outline into this scene list: "Take this idea—'a young widow becomes a smuggler during the French Revolution'—and turn it into 15 scenes with emotional stakes," or "Build a scene list for a historical drama set during the Great Fire of London." Get those building blocks down fast. You're not writing yet. You're mapping the path so that when you begin, you never stop to wonder, *what next?*

Once you have your outline, commit to a rough schedule. It could look something like this: one hour of prep, six to eight hours of focused writing sprints, and a final hour or two for reading through, tightening dialogue, and checking pacing. Use a timer. Turn off distractions. This isn't just about speed—it's about sustained immersion. The more deeply you stay in the world of your story, the more naturally the words will come.

Start with a *fast, visceral opening scene*. Set the tone. Give your main character something to react to—a threat, a loss, a sight they weren't supposed to see. Don't explain the world. Let the atmosphere, tension, and action *show* the historical setting. Ask ChatGPT, "Give me a vivid first paragraph for a story set during the Armenian genocide," or "Write a tense first scene for a character arriving in plague-stricken Florence in 1348."

Once you've nailed that opening, don't stop to edit. Keep moving through your scene list. Each scene should revolve around a *conflict or emotional beat*. Dialogue, action, and description should all serve that beat. If the scene is about betrayal, let every line of dialogue crack with suspicion or false comfort. If it's about courage, build the fear first, then the decision.

Any time you hit a wall, outsource it. Ask ChatGPT to draft a dialogue exchange, describe a setting, or summarize the next scene in your outline. Say, "Write a confrontation between a suffragette and her aristocratic father in 1908 London," or "Describe a marketplace in Damascus during the Ottoman Empire." You're not replacing your voice—you're feeding it with fuel so the engine doesn't stall.

Remember to keep your story *anchored in character*. Each historical beat—each war, riot, treaty, or invention—only matters if it changes someone on the page. Don't explain the politics. Show how they hit someone's heart. The beauty of writing fast is that you write instinctively, emotionally. You let the story breathe through people, not textbooks. If you stay close to your characters' fears, desires, and decisions, the history becomes real, urgent, and alive.

Halfway through the day, pause to check your emotional arc. Are you building tension? Are your characters evolving? Has something shifted since page one? If not, intensify your next few scenes. Raise the stakes. Add a betrayal, a twist, or a moral dilemma. Ask ChatGPT to brainstorm: "What plot twist could break two sisters apart during the French occupation of Algeria?" or "How might a letter from the front lines change a mother's plan to flee occupied Poland?"

When you reach the final act, write like you're rolling downhill. This is where the consequences hit. Your climax doesn't have to be loud—but it has to be inevitable. A secret exposed. A sacrifice made. A choice that echoes back to the beginning. Let it happen fast and raw. Don't slow down to make it perfect. Just land the emotion. You can always refine later.

As you write your final scene, think of image, gesture, or silence. Let it *feel* like an ending, not just a stopping point. Ask ChatGPT for help if you want something powerful: "What's a symbolic final scene for a woman who escaped slavery and sees her daughter speak freely for the first time?" or "Give me a quiet ending that reflects the cost of war on a soldier returning home in 1919."

Once you're done, take a short break—then read through your draft. You're not editing for grammar. You're checking for flow. Are the emotional beats hitting? Are the scenes moving forward? If something feels slow or unclear, jot a note. But don't get bogged down. Just patch it enough to feel complete.

And when you finish, take a moment. You've done something most writers dream of: you've pulled a complete historical drama out of the air and brought it into being. Not just words on a page—but a world, full of breath and memory, anchored in the past but vibrating with life.

From outline to final draft, in a single day.

It's not a shortcut—it's a creative sprint, a trust fall into history, and proof that with focus and the right tools, the impossible is absolutely within reach.

Using ChatGPT to Edit and Expand Your Historical Draft

You've done it—you've written a full draft of your historical drama. Whether it took a day or a month, you now have characters, a setting, and a plot that you've wrestled into shape. But a first draft, by nature, is only the beginning. It's the bones. The breath. The heartbeat. Now it needs clarity, texture, and polish. This is where ChatGPT becomes one of your most powerful creative tools—not just to edit typos or rephrase clunky lines, but to help you **expand**, deepen, and refine every corner of your story.

Think of ChatGPT not as a red-pen editor, but as a collaborator who can hold a mirror up to your draft and say, "Here's what's working. Here's what's not. And here's how to take it further."

Start with a global read. Copy and paste a full scene—or even the entire draft, depending on length—and ask ChatGPT for a **broad critique**. Try prompts like, "What's missing emotionally from this scene?" or "What could make the pacing stronger in this chapter?" You're not asking for judgment. You're looking for insight—neutral, structured, and free from ego. It won't sugarcoat. It will offer precise feedback like, "The scene begins with tension but loses momentum halfway through," or "Consider clarifying the protagonist's goal here."

Then go granular. Focus on **individual character arcs**. Ask, "Does my protagonist change clearly from beginning to end?" or "Does the antagonist feel one-dimensional, and how can I make them more layered?" ChatGPT can suggest ways to humanize a villain or reveal internal conflict in a stoic hero. If you've written a subplot that feels flat, try, "How can I deepen the emotional tension between these two characters during this time period?"

You can also run **dialogue clean-ups**. Paste in lines that feel awkward, stiff, or too modern, and ask, "Make this conversation sound more natural for 18th-century Scotland," or "Rewrite this so it's sharper and more emotionally charged." You can even ask ChatGPT to **add subtext**: "Make this dialogue about political betrayal, but don't have the characters say it outright." Watch how the lines tighten, the silences speak, and the emotional tension grows.

When it comes to **expanding scenes**, ChatGPT is incredibly effective. Maybe you have a bare-bones dinner scene. Ask, "What historical details can I add to make this dinner in 1930s Berlin feel richer?" It might suggest background sounds, food choices, newspaper headlines on the table, and clothing that reflects both character and setting. These aren't just decorations—they're immersive tools.

Let's say a chapter ends too abruptly. Ask ChatGPT, "Add 100 more words that deepen the protagonist's internal reaction to the scene without changing what happens." This approach ensures the expansion serves the emotion, not just the word count.

You can also do this with **transition scenes**, which often get rushed in historical stories. Traveling from city to city, or jumping forward a year, needs more than a sentence if it's meant to carry emotional weight. Try, "Create a visual and emotional paragraph that shows the journey from Paris to the Spanish border in 1812 after the main character has just lost their brother." It will give you a passage that blends setting, mood, and reflection—exactly what's needed to maintain story rhythm.

Another powerful use of ChatGPT in revision is to **check historical consistency**. Ask, "Does this scene align with what someone in 1885 London would realistically say or do?" or "What mistakes am I making in portraying the Ottoman Empire in 1914?" It's not a substitute for deep research, but it's a fantastic tool for flagging anything that might ring false or need more support.

If your story is too exposition-heavy, use prompts like, "How can I reveal this information about 17th-century Dutch politics through action instead of narration?" Or, "Give me a historical metaphor that a peasant in medieval France might use to explain betrayal." It'll help you replace dry info-dumps with character-driven storytelling.

And if you're feeling stuck or unsure about rewriting a whole scene, you can literally say, "Take this scene and rewrite it with higher emotional intensity and clearer stakes." ChatGPT will deliver a revised version, often showing you what you already had in your head—but hadn't quite figured out how to express.

As you revise your draft scene by scene, ChatGPT also helps you **track emotional arcs** and **highlight themes**. Ask, "How well does this chapter reinforce my theme of legacy versus loss?" or "Where in this dialogue could I echo the idea of silence as survival?" These thematic refinements are subtle but powerful. They take your draft from being a historical story to a resonant, layered narrative.

Use ChatGPT to test endings, too. "Give me three alternative versions of the ending that feel historically plausible but emotionally different—one hopeful, one tragic, and one ambiguous." You may find one of those endings says exactly what your story needs to say.

Lastly, remember that revision is not just about cleaning up—it's about **re-discovering** your story. ChatGPT doesn't take the story away from you. It gives you new ways to see it, feel it, shape it. It offers perspective without fatigue, inspiration without ego, and solutions without delay.

So when you're ready to edit and expand, don't stare at your screen alone.

Ask questions. Test ideas. Try rewrites.

Let your draft breathe new life.

Because with the right prompts and an open mind, ChatGPT isn't just an editor.

It's your historian. Your scene partner. Your quiet, ever-curious co-writer.

Testing Your Story for Accuracy and Heart

Finishing a historical drama draft is a huge achievement, but before you consider it truly *finished*, there are two vital questions you need to ask: Is it **accurate**, and does it have **heart**? These two pillars—truth and feeling—are what transform a collection of scenes into a living, breathing story. One anchors your work in a believable, immersive world. The other gives it emotional resonance. Without accuracy, your story falls flat. Without heart, it won't be remembered. So how do you test for both?

Start with **historical accuracy**, not to chase perfection, but to build trust with your audience. Your reader or viewer may not know every detail of 12th-century Florence or 19th-century Bengal, but they can *feel* when something's off. A single modern phrase, an anachronistic object, or a cultural misstep can break the illusion you've worked so hard to create. This doesn't mean you have to be rigid or academic—it just means you need to create a world that feels internally consistent, respectful of its context, and grounded in research.

To test this, go through your draft and flag anything that feels too modern, vague, or overly simplified. Then ask ChatGPT questions like, "Would this phrase exist in 1790s France?" or "What would a typical breakfast look like in Edo-era Japan?" You can even ask for a scene-by-scene scan: "Review this chapter and point out any historical inaccuracies or anachronisms." You'll likely uncover small things—terminology, behavior, societal roles—that can be fixed easily, but make a big difference in immersion.

Accuracy also applies to **behavior and mindset**. Characters should think, react, and speak according to the norms, beliefs, and limitations of their time. That doesn't mean they can't challenge those norms, but their worldview needs to be shaped by the world they live in. If a Victorian woman in your story has radical ideas about gender, that's fine—just give her a reason. Ground her thinking in experience, exposure, or inner conflict. Let her journey be real, not a modern projection.

You can test this by prompting ChatGPT: "Would a middle-class woman in 1850s Boston realistically have these political opinions?" or "What would be the internal conflict for a samurai who begins to question the shogunate?" Use the answers not as limits, but as story enhancers. The closer you get to historical plausibility, the richer your characters become.

Once you've reviewed your story for factual grounding, turn your attention to its **heart**—the emotional core that holds everything together. This isn't about being sentimental. It's about ensuring that each scene carries emotional purpose, that each character matters, and that the story says something *true* about the human experience.

To test this, take a step back and ask, "What is my story really about?" If your answer is something like, "The Irish War of Independence," you're missing the heart. But if it's, "A father trying to protect his children as the world around him falls apart," now you're closer. That emotional throughline should pulse beneath every historical event, shaping how you write it and why your audience will care.

Ask yourself: Do my characters change? Do they feel real pain, joy, fear, guilt, longing? Are they just reacting to events, or are they *struggling with something personal* at every stage of the plot? If you're not sure, ask ChatGPT: "What is the emotional arc of this character based on this summary?" or "Which scenes deepen the relationship between these two characters?" You'll get clear insights into whether your emotional beats are hitting—or if they need more space to breathe.

Another way to test for heart is to zoom in on **individual scenes**. Pick your key moments—your turning points, climaxes, quiet pauses—and ask, "What is the emotional center of this scene?" If you can't answer clearly, that scene might need more work. A revolution without heartbreak, a death without reflection, a kiss without risk—those are missed opportunities.

Use ChatGPT to dig deeper: "Rewrite this scene to emphasize the character's grief without adding dialogue," or "What physical actions could show repressed anger in this confrontation?" Sometimes heart doesn't come from words, but from pauses, touches, absences. Sometimes it's what your characters don't say that carries the weight.

Don't be afraid to **cut scenes** that don't serve either history or emotion. Just because something is interesting doesn't mean it's necessary. Ask, "What would happen if I removed this chapter?" If the story still holds, it might be filler. Trim away anything that slows the emotional rhythm or muddies the historical arc. Then look for moments that feel thin—and *expand them with purpose*. You can prompt ChatGPT: "Add 100 words to this scene to heighten the tension between mother and son," or "Give this moment a symbolic image that underscores the theme of loss."

And finally, share your work. Give it to readers who know the history—and some who don't. Ask them both: Did it feel *real*? Did it *move* you? Use their feedback to refine, not to retreat. ChatGPT can help interpret reader notes, identify common critiques, and suggest fixes without overwriting your voice.

Because testing for accuracy and heart isn't about ticking boxes.

It's about honoring the past and connecting it to the present. It's about building a world that feels lived in—and filling it with characters who feel alive.

And when your story rings true both in fact and feeling, you haven't just written historical drama.

You've written something that will stand the test of time.

Writing Your Historical Drama with Confidence and Speed

Writing historical drama can feel like trying to steer a ship through fog—you're navigating a world built on facts, dates, traditions, and expectations, all while chasing the emotional truth of your characters. It's no wonder writers sometimes freeze at the start, second-guess themselves mid-draft, and spend weeks researching the color of a dress or the breed of a horse. But if your goal is to write your historical drama with both **confidence** and **speed**, then you need to embrace a new mindset—one that blends intuition, structure, and creative flow with smart use of tools like ChatGPT to move you forward rather than slow you down.

Confidence comes from knowing what matters *most*. Speed comes from letting go of what doesn't.

Before you write a single word, define your **emotional core**. What's this story *really* about? Not the setting, not the event, not the time period—but the feeling at its center. A daughter trying to forgive her mother. A man carrying guilt through war. A rebel who wants to be heard. When you know the emotional thread, you can write with direction. No matter how deep into history your story goes, your characters will lead you through it.

Once that core is clear, **build a simple roadmap**. You don't need a 40-page outline. Just list 10 to 15 major emotional or plot beats—turning points, decisions, shifts, discoveries. These are your waypoints. They let you focus scene by scene, never losing track of the destination. If you're writing a screenplay, break your beats into three acts. If it's a novel, sketch the rise, fall, and resolution of your central relationship or conflict. Use ChatGPT to help lay this out: "Give me 12 emotionally driven plot points for a story about a teenage soldier during the Napoleonic Wars."

Once you begin writing, treat **momentum** as sacred. Don't stop to check facts in the middle of a sentence. Don't break the emotional rhythm to confirm whether a cathedral existed in 1356. If something trips you up, make a quick note—[confirm if accurate]—and keep going. Trust that you can layer in the details later. What matters in the first draft is emotion, structure, and voice.

Use ChatGPT as your *first responder*. Got a blank page? Say, "Write a tense opening scene where a family hides in a crypt during the French Revolution." Need description? Ask, "Give me the sights and sounds of a port city in the Ottoman Empire." Stuck in dialogue? Try, "Write a scene where a widow confronts the soldier who killed her husband, but they're both pretending not to know."

The key is to **ask smart, targeted questions**. ChatGPT won't write your entire story for you—but it will help you keep your fingers moving, your ideas flowing, and your scenes alive.

Speed doesn't mean rushing—it means **not hesitating**. Don't rewrite your first paragraph five times. Don't spend an hour naming a minor character. Don't overthink tone, punctuation, or scene transitions. Those are editing problems. First drafts are about laying bricks, not painting the walls. Write fast. Write freely. Write as if someone's burning your notes tomorrow.

Confidence grows as you **see the pages pile up**. The more you write, the more the story reveals itself. You don't need to know everything before you start. In fact, some of your best discoveries come mid-sentence. A quiet reaction becomes a major turning point. A one-line side character steals a scene. Let those moments in. Let the story breathe. Then go back and strengthen the structure.

Use **historical texture** to elevate your scenes, but don't drown in it. One vivid detail—a coat buttoned with trembling hands, a protest chant echoing in the distance, a coal fire hissing in a silent room—can transport the reader more than a full page of description. Ask ChatGPT for specific textures when needed: "What kind of shoes would a Polish resistance fighter wear in 1944?" or "Describe the feeling of sitting in a Mongol yurt during winter."

If you start feeling overwhelmed—too many facts, too many characters, too much pressure to get it "right"—pull back to the **human element**. What is your character feeling right now? What are they afraid of? What do they want that they cannot have? These questions keep you grounded. They give your story urgency and soul.

And don't forget the power of **ritual and routine**. Set a timer for 25 minutes and commit to writing without stopping. Use ChatGPT to spark ideas before each sprint. Start your writing day by generating a prompt like, "Write 300 words where a soldier hears music in the middle of battle," or "Begin a scene where a royal is about to be dethroned but has one final conversation with a servant." These mini-exercises keep your creativity sharp and your story moving.

In the end, writing historical drama quickly and confidently is about **trust**. Trust your emotional instincts. Trust the arc of your story. Trust that your revisions will take care of the rest. And trust that tools like ChatGPT are not crutches—they're creative accelerators. They help you skip the hesitation phase and go straight to storytelling.

So write boldly. Write fast. Write like you've lived this life before.

Because when you stop doubting, start asking, and just *begin*—

you'll discover that confidence isn't something you wait for.

It's something you write your way into, one scene at a time.

Examples of Prompts for Historical Drama Story Design and Structure

When writing historical drama, the quality of your story often depends on the quality of your questions. A well-crafted prompt doesn't just spark creativity—it *guides* it. It's your flashlight into the past, helping you shape your story with precision, imagination, and emotional depth. Whether you're working with ChatGPT or brainstorming solo, good prompts help you zero in on character arcs, plot tension, thematic weight, and historical texture. They move you past surface-level research and into the marrow of your narrative.

Here are examples of high-impact prompts organized by purpose to help you design and structure your historical drama with purpose, clarity, and speed.

Prompts for Generating Story Ideas and Conflict

- "Give me a story idea set in 15th-century Spain that centers on a forbidden relationship between people from two different faiths."
- "What kind of conflict could arise between a former soldier and a young revolutionary in post-Napoleonic France?"
- "Give me three emotionally charged plot ideas involving a midwife during the Black Plague."
- "Design a story set in 1920s Shanghai that explores identity, betrayal, and political tension."

These types of prompts set you up with foundational story elements that are already steeped in setting, theme, and emotional stakes.

Prompts for Character Development in Historical Contexts

- "Create a character profile for a female spy in 1940s Berlin who works against her own government."
- "What internal conflict would a Japanese samurai face during the transition from feudalism to modernity in the Meiji era?"
- "Describe a character who is a closeted gay writer in 1950s America and how the political climate affects their decisions."
- "What fears, ambitions, and secrets would a 17-year-old servant have in a Tudor palace?"

These prompts encourage rich, layered protagonists and side characters shaped by time, place, and pressure.

Prompts for Structuring the Plot

- "Give me a three-act structure for a historical drama about a royal cook caught up in palace intrigue."
- "Outline the plot beats for a story set during the fall of Constantinople, told from the perspective of a teenage apprentice."
- "Break this story concept into 12 scenes: a runaway bride in 19th-century India becomes a spiritual healer in exile."
- "How would a dual-timeline structure work in a story set in ancient Rome and modern-day Italy, centered on a family heirloom?"

These are highly useful when you have a story idea and want to put it into motion quickly.

Prompts for Building Authentic Historical Settings

- "Describe a busy street in Cairo in 1800: sounds, smells, people, and atmosphere."
- "What would a prison in 16th-century England look and feel like from the point of view of a political prisoner?"
- "What rituals and daily routines would define life for a nun in 14th-century France?"
- "Build a setting inside a crumbling Russian manor during the Bolshevik Revolution."

When your setting feels real, your scenes feel grounded—and prompts like these bring that reality forward.

Prompts for Emotional Beats and Thematic Weight

- "What small gesture can show a mother's grief after losing a child in a war she never believed in?"
- "Give me a quiet, emotional scene between two friends who are about to fight on opposite sides of a civil war."
- "How can I show the theme of silence as resistance in a story set during the Spanish Inquisition?"
- "What metaphor could tie a story together about generational trauma in a Jewish family before, during, and after the Holocaust?"

These kinds of prompts elevate your story from event-based to meaning-based.

Prompts for Writing Specific Types of Scenes

- "Write a tense courtroom scene in 17th-century Salem where a character is falsely accused of witchcraft."
- "Describe a romantic farewell at a train station in 1942 as a soldier departs for war."
- "Create a dinner table scene in Renaissance Florence where political betrayal is hinted at but never spoken."
- "Write a silent scene between a man and his wife after he returns from years of exile."

These prompts help build scenes that are emotionally and structurally vital to your story.

Prompts for Revisions and Expansions

- "How can I rewrite this scene to make the emotional stakes clearer without changing the plot?"
- "Add more historical detail to this marketplace scene in 1800s New Orleans."
- "Suggest a way to show my protagonist's guilt more strongly in this confrontation."
- "What could I insert between chapters three and four to deepen the relationship between these two characters?"

Use prompts like these when you're tightening or expanding a draft and want fresh perspective.

Prompts for Framing and Structure Devices

- "What would a framing device look like if I started with a modern historian discovering a journal from the past?"
- "Give me a prologue idea for a story about a child who will grow up to start a rebellion."

- “Suggest a way to use flashbacks to reveal the truth about a betrayal that happened 20 years before the story begins.”
- “How can I end my story in the present day while honoring the events of the past without being preachy?”

These help you layer narrative structure without breaking the historical immersion.

Prompts for Enhancing Subtext and Symbolism

- “What recurring image could symbolize freedom in a story set in colonial Haiti?”
- “What silent behaviors would show someone’s guilt after turning in a loved one to the Gestapo?”
- “How can I show two characters are in love without them saying it, in a time when their love is illegal?”
- “Suggest a subtle motif that could be woven through a story about exile and return.”

Subtext makes historical fiction feel more intelligent, more human, and more enduring—and prompts can help sharpen that focus.

In the end, a good prompt doesn’t just generate content. It generates *vision*. It keeps you aligned with the emotional arc, historical context, and narrative structure all at once. When you find yourself stuck or slowed down, lean on prompts. Use them to open doors that logic can’t always knock on.

Because the real secret to writing a brilliant historical drama isn’t just knowing your history.

It’s knowing the *right questions* to ask of it.

Examples of Prompts for Designing Historical Drama Characters

When it comes to historical drama, your characters are more than just participants in a bygone era—they are the lens through which the past becomes personal. A compelling historical character isn't just accurate to their time period—they're emotionally layered, driven by human needs, trapped by their circumstances, and challenged by change. Designing characters who feel real, relevant, and resonant begins with asking the right questions. Whether you're brainstorming from scratch or deepening someone already on the page, prompts are your most effective tool for pulling complexity out of the shadows.

Below is a curated guide to high-impact prompts for designing unforgettable characters in historical settings—organized by purpose, so you can spark depth, conflict, and emotion as you build your cast.

Prompts for Building Rich Historical Backstories

- "Create a detailed backstory for a young widow in 1916 who has just inherited her husband's failing bookstore in Lisbon."
- "Who might a former slave become 20 years after Emancipation, and how would they view freedom differently than others in their community?"
- "What kind of life would a teenage girl in 15th-century Kyoto have if her mother was a respected poet and her father was a disgraced nobleman?"
- "Describe the early childhood of a boy born into a plague doctor's family in 1600s Venice."

These prompts root your character in their world—giving them a personal history as complex as the time period they inhabit.

Prompts for Identifying Core Motivations and Emotional Drives

- "What does a Catholic nun in 1890s Ireland want more than anything—and what is she afraid it might cost her?"
- "Why would a Mongolian horse trainer in the 13th century secretly want to escape his own clan?"
- "What guilt drives a retired Civil War soldier now living in a quiet Pennsylvania town in 1875?"
- "What would compel a seamstress in Revolutionary France to spy for the monarchy, even if she believes in the people's cause?"

Great characters don't exist in neutrality—they live in contradiction. These questions pull out those contradictions.

Prompts for Character Flaws, Secrets, and Inner Conflict

- "What does a decorated WWI nurse lie about in every job interview, and why can't she forgive herself?"
- "Create a character in ancient Sparta who is physically strong but emotionally fragile—and hide that tension in their daily routine."
- "What secret is a wealthy merchant hiding from his family in 1800s Shanghai, and how does that secret inform his decisions?"
- "What inner shame drives a 1950s jazz musician who was once a child prodigy in a small Southern church?"

Every historical figure has a public face and a private reality. These prompts help peel away the armor.

Prompts for Character Relationships

- "Design a relationship between a father and daughter in 1840s New Orleans, where the father is part of the underground resistance and the daughter wants nothing to do with rebellion."
- "Create two childhood friends on opposite sides of the Irish Civil War, still tied by a shared trauma from their youth."
- "Describe a forbidden romance between a plantation owner's wife and a teacher from the North who has come to educate the freedmen."
- "What's the dynamic between a chambermaid and the noblewoman she serves in 18th-century Russia?"

Relationships are where history becomes emotional. These prompts help you explore tension, affection, betrayal, and longing within the social structures of the time.

Prompts for Cultural and Social Context

- "What role does religion play in the daily life of a Jewish bookseller in 1930s Poland?"
- "How would caste affect the worldview and self-worth of a potter's apprentice in 18th-century India?"
- "What moral values would guide a Confucian scholar in the Joseon Dynasty, and how would those values be tested?"
- "What biases and blind spots would a white suffragette in 1912 likely have—and how could those affect her arc?"

Characters aren't just shaped by their personal history—they're shaped by *social* history. These prompts help you embed those forces into their psyche.

Prompts for Creating Symbolic or Archetypal Characters

- "Create a character who represents the dying spirit of an old empire—but doesn't realize it until it's too late."
- "Write a character who embodies resistance, but only through silence."
- "Design a tragic figure whose dream of progress ends up destroying everything they love."
- "Build a character who is an outsider in every way—language, culture, belief—but becomes the conscience of the story."

These prompts help you design characters that carry *thematic weight*, connecting the personal to the universal.

Prompts for Characters at a Turning Point

- "What is the moral line a 19th-century abolitionist is afraid to cross, and what pushes them over it?"
- "How does a respected Chinese general in the Ming Dynasty come to question everything he was taught about loyalty?"
- "What moment causes a loyal samurai to betray his master—and how does he live with it afterward?"
- "Describe the moment a peasant woman in a medieval English village chooses to hide a fugitive monk."

Turning points reveal who people *really* are. These prompts shine a light on the critical moments that reshape characters forever.

Prompts for Minor Characters Who Matter

- "Who is the gravedigger in a plague-ravaged French town—and what is he doing with the bodies at night?"
- "Describe the daily life of the midwife who helps both the wealthy and the poor—but hears every secret in the process."
- "Create a silent boy who sweeps the floors of a prison and knows every guard's weakness."
- "Write the perspective of the servant who overhears the conspiracy but cannot read or write."

Minor characters become memorable when they hold secrets, bear witness, or quietly move the story in unseen ways. These prompts make them matter.

Prompts to Use ChatGPT as Your Character Design Partner

- "Help me build a character arc for a disillusioned priest during the Spanish Civil War."
- "I want a character in 1920s Harlem who is both a jazz musician and a Communist sympathizer. Help me build their fears and ambitions."
- "Give me three possible character motivations for a sailor on a slave ship who eventually turns against the captain."
- "What kind of emotional wound would drive a woman in ancient Egypt to pose as a man to study science?"

With well-designed prompts, ChatGPT becomes not just a tool for generation—but a partner in complexity.

Historical drama isn't about recreating the past. It's about letting characters *live* through it. Their fears, their decisions, their regrets and hopes—that's where history becomes *story*. The better your characters, the deeper the emotional impact of your historical setting.

So write characters who are shaped by their world, but not defined by it. Ask big questions. Dig deep. And let your characters carry the emotional truth of their time.

Because when your characters are real, the past isn't distant.

It's unforgettable.

Examples of Prompts for World-Building in Historical Dramas

World-building is often associated with fantasy and science fiction, but it's just as essential in historical drama—because the past is its own strange world. A world where the rules were different, the rhythms were slower, the values and fears unfamiliar. The goal of historical world-building is to make a long-gone era feel immediate and lived-in—not just described from the outside, but *felt* from within. And the most effective way to do that, especially with the help of tools like ChatGPT, is by asking the right **prompts** to flesh out your story's geography, culture, politics, atmosphere, and sensory details.

The following prompts are grouped by purpose, giving you a toolkit to construct rich, immersive worlds that are authentic, emotionally charged, and tailor-made for storytelling.

Prompts for Designing Locations with Specific Atmosphere

- "Describe a fog-drenched fishing village on the English coast in 1845 during a cholera outbreak."
- "Create a vivid scene of a bustling spice market in 16th-century Constantinople through the senses of a young thief."
- "What would a noble family estate in Prussia look and feel like on the eve of World War I?"
- "Write the layout and mood of a monastery in medieval Ireland during a time of political unrest."

These prompts help you paint places not just visually, but emotionally—setting the tone for your characters' experiences.

Prompts for Social and Cultural Texture

- "What traditions and customs would shape daily life for a middle-class family in Edo-era Japan?"
- "List the religious practices of an Ethiopian Orthodox Christian village in the 1800s and how they affect the weekly calendar."
- "What rites of passage would a young woman go through in 12th-century Mali?"
- "What are the unspoken rules of class behavior at a French aristocrat's dinner table in 1788?"

Culture is more than just surface detail—it's what shapes every choice your characters make. These prompts help you build social fabric.

Prompts for Government, Law, and Power Structures

- "Explain how power is maintained and passed on in a tribal kingdom in pre-colonial Africa."
- "What legal restrictions would a merchant face in Qing Dynasty China when trying to expand his business?"
- "Describe how a revolutionary government maintains order in 1793 Paris and what punishments are feared most."
- "Who enforces the law in a small town in the American West in 1871, and what forms of justice are unofficial but accepted?"

These prompts help you build the systems that create conflict and determine the stakes in your story world.

Prompts for Class, Labor, and Economy

- "What jobs would be available to orphaned girls in 1830s Manchester during the height of the textile boom?"
- "How would a spice merchant in 1400s Venice rise in status, and who would oppose him?"
- "What was the daily grind like for dock workers in colonial Havana—and how did they survive between paydays?"
- "Describe the economy of a Scottish highland village during a potato famine, and how bartering shaped relationships."

Economics shape opportunity, desperation, and rebellion. These prompts help you understand how people *lived*—and struggled.

Prompts for Domestic and Daily Life

- "Describe the contents of a family home in 1700s Mexico City—furniture, tools, lighting, and decoration."
- "What did a typical breakfast look like for an upper-class woman in 19th-century Vienna versus her servant?"
- "What daily routines would a knight's squire follow in medieval England, from dawn to dusk?"
- "What games did children play in the streets of Renaissance Florence, and what stories did they tell each other?"

Daily life breathes realism into your scenes. These prompts ensure you can move through your world as if you live there.

Prompts for Architecture, Clothing, and Material Culture

- "What would the fashion of a rebellious young woman in 1920s Berlin look like, and what would it signal to others?"
- "Describe the design, lighting, and feeling of a Moorish palace at sunset in 13th-century Andalusia."
- "What type of armor would a Persian warrior wear in the 6th century, and how would it affect his movement?"
- "What kinds of tools and utensils would you find in a Viking-era kitchen, and how would meals be prepared?"

These help you enrich your story with visual texture—objects, buildings, and attire that ground your characters in time.

Prompts for Religion, Belief Systems, and Superstition

- "What spiritual practices would shape the day of a priestess in ancient Mesopotamia?"
- "How would an Irish farmer in 1847 interpret a solar eclipse—and what rituals might follow?"
- "What tensions exist between traditional beliefs and colonial religion in 19th-century Kenya?"
- "Describe the daily prayers, omens, and taboos that govern the life of a Roman legionary."

Belief systems affect love, war, work, and justice. These prompts open a doorway into how characters understand life and death.

Prompts for Events and Historical Moments

- "Create the atmosphere in the streets of St. Petersburg the day after the Russian Revolution begins."
- "What would a refugee camp look like along the Silk Road during a major Mongol invasion?"
- "Describe the feeling in a town square in New Orleans on the day slavery was abolished."
- "What rumors would ripple through a Scottish village the week before the Battle of Culloden?"

Moments of crisis or transition are rich storytelling territory. These prompts help you capture a turning point in immersive detail.

Prompts for Multi-Sensory Immersion

- "Describe the smells, textures, and sounds of a Bedouin tent city at sunrise in the 1800s."
- "What does it feel like to walk through the muddy streets of a 17th-century London slum in winter?"
- "Imagine a formal banquet in an imperial Chinese court—describe it from the point of view of a hungry servant."
- "Describe the physical discomforts of traveling across medieval Europe on horseback in the dead of winter."

The more senses you activate, the more your world becomes *real*. These prompts go beyond sight and into full immersion.

Prompts for World-Building through Contrast

- "Describe the difference between an aristocrat's and a servant's bedroom in an 18th-century Polish manor house."
- "What rules apply in the public bathhouses of Istanbul, and how does gender affect the experience?"
- "Contrast a rural farming village with a port city in colonial Brazil from the perspective of a teenage boy."
- "Describe a Jewish child's experience of Sabbath in a large European city versus a small shtetl in 1900."

These side-by-side contrasts create nuance and tension, highlighting inequality, power, and cultural variation.

Prompts to Use ChatGPT as a World-Building Assistant

- "Give me five historically accurate world-building elements for a story set in the Ottoman Empire in 1560."
- "Build a detailed map description of a fictional port city inspired by 1700s Portugal."
- "Help me invent cultural customs for a fictional tribe inspired by real African communities during the 1700s."
- "What objects would you find in a typical barracks for Roman soldiers stationed in Gaul?"

ChatGPT becomes your world-building partner—bringing quick research, vivid description, and layered complexity on demand.

World-building isn't just a backdrop—it's the *soul* of your historical drama. It's what shapes the decisions your characters make, the battles they fight, the dreams they chase, and the cages they live in.

Ask boldly. Imagine deeply. Build wisely.

Because when your world is fully alive, your story becomes something unforgettable—history not just studied, but *felt*.

Examples of Prompts for Ideas about Historical Drama Stories

Coming up with compelling ideas for a historical drama doesn't mean you need to be a scholar or memorize dates. It just means you need the right *questions*. Great historical stories often begin not with an era, but with a *feeling*—injustice, hope, love, betrayal, resistance. Then that feeling gets wrapped in time, place, and circumstance. With the right prompts, you can generate endless story ideas that are both historically rich and emotionally powerful.

Below is a curated list of high-impact prompts to help you brainstorm fresh, dramatic, and meaningful historical story ideas—whether you want to write a novel, a short story, a screenplay, or a series.

Prompts for Character-Driven Historical Dramas

- "Give me a story idea about a young servant who witnesses a political assassination in 16th-century Florence."
- "Create a historical drama about a female doctor hiding her identity during the American Civil War."
- "Give me a love story between a Japanese artist and a Dutch merchant during Japan's isolationist Edo period."
- "Suggest a plot for a former slave who returns to the South to find their family after the Civil War."

These prompts start with human stakes and emotions, then unfold in rich historical settings.

Prompts Focused on Conflict and Upheaval

- "What's a story set during the fall of Constantinople, told from the perspective of a teenage boy trapped inside the city?"
- "Give me a dramatic story about a woman accused of witchcraft in Puritan New England who hides a revolutionary secret."
- "Create a plot involving two brothers on opposing sides during the Spanish Civil War."
- "Describe a story that unfolds during the Partition of India through the eyes of a train conductor."

Conflict is the heart of drama—these prompts embed it directly into explosive historical events.

Prompts for Stories about Hidden Histories and Silenced Voices

- "Tell me a story about an enslaved midwife in 1800s Brazil who uses herbs and whispers to protect her people."
- "Give me a plot centered on a deaf child growing up in 1930s Harlem who becomes an underground poet."
- "What's a historical drama about a forgotten female pirate who ruled a South China Sea port in the 1700s?"
- "Write a story about a queer love affair hidden inside a Catholic monastery during the Spanish Inquisition."

These prompts help you uncover the untold, the hidden, and the emotionally urgent stories that history books often miss.

Prompts That Combine Two Unusual Elements

- "Create a story that combines the invention of the printing press with a secret society of women scribes."
- "Write a story about a child who is the illegitimate offspring of an emperor and is raised by nomads."
- "Imagine a historical drama about an aging gladiator who becomes a pacifist after witnessing a divine sign."
- "Design a story where a plague doctor falls in love with the ghost of someone they couldn't save."

Combining elements—love, mysticism, technology, espionage—with historical drama creates unique and unforgettable narratives.

Prompts for Political and Revolutionary Stories

- "Give me a historical drama about a failed uprising told entirely from the point of view of the prison cook."
- "Write a plot involving a royal advisor who starts leaking secrets to revolutionaries in 18th-century France."
- "What's a story about a child smuggler who helps people escape the Berlin Wall in the early 1960s?"
- "Tell me a story about a printing press owner who hides banned texts during the Cultural Revolution in China."

These stories are about ideology, danger, and transformation—fertile ground for bold drama.

Prompts for Multi-Generational or Dual-Timeline Dramas

- "Give me a story that follows three generations of a Black family in Mississippi, from slavery to the Civil Rights Movement."
- "Write a dual-timeline story about a woman in WWII Germany and her granddaughter uncovering the truth decades later."
- "Create a story that begins with a Viking raid and ends with a modern archaeologist discovering the truth."
- "Describe a family saga that spans from the Opium Wars to present-day Hong Kong."

These prompts allow for scope, depth, and emotional resonance across time.

Prompts with a Focus on Everyday People during Big Moments

- "Tell me a story about a baker in Paris during the Reign of Terror who hides refugees in the back of his shop."
- "What happens when a shepherd in 1940s Greece finds a downed Allied pilot?"
- "Write about a blind piano tuner who becomes a spy during World War I."
- "Create a historical drama centered around a nurse during the Irish Famine who risks her job to save children."

Sometimes it's the ordinary people—not the kings and generals—who give history its deepest humanity.

Prompts for Stories Built Around Specific Objects or Events

- "What's the story of a wedding ring passed down from a Holocaust survivor that ends up in a pawn shop in 1980s New York?"
- "Create a drama about the woman who painted a famous propaganda poster during WWII—and the

secret behind the image."

- "Tell me a story about a soldier's diary that is discovered in a trench, half-buried for a century."
- "Write a plot based on a pair of shoes recovered from the Titanic wreckage."

Objects can carry history, emotion, and secrets—they're excellent anchors for story development.

Prompts for Stories with Psychological and Emotional Complexity

- "Write a historical drama about a war survivor who returns home only to find their identity stolen."
- "Tell a story of a nobleman who pretends to be mad to avoid execution during the English Civil War."
- "Describe a young mother hiding her PTSD in a post-WWI Italian village that has no name for trauma."
- "Create a story about a child who grows up thinking they were abandoned—until they discover the truth through a letter found in a church."

These stories are rich with emotion, moral complexity, and personal stakes.

Prompts to Use with ChatGPT for Fast, Specific Story Ideas

- "Give me five story concepts set in 19th-century Istanbul that involve betrayal and redemption."
- "Suggest a plot where a female character in ancient Rome must escape both political persecution and arranged marriage."
- "Help me design a story with a character arc that mirrors the collapse of the British Empire."
- "List story ideas set in West Africa between 1600–1800 with emotional character conflict at the center."

Let ChatGPT do the heavy lifting when you're brainstorming and want options fast and tailored to theme, setting, or character.

A great historical drama story idea doesn't start with, "What year was this battle?" It starts with a whisper of *emotion*, a moment of *moral tension*, a choice with no easy answer. Then you let the setting build around it like flesh on bone.

Use prompts to unlock those sparks. Twist them. Deepen them. Make them your own.

Because the past is full of voices waiting to speak.

All you need to do is ask the right question.

Repeat and Improve – Becoming a Prolific Writer

Prolific writers aren't born—they're built. They don't wait for inspiration, and they don't rely on luck. Instead, they master the art of **showing up**, using systems that allow them to create consistently and improve continuously. When it comes to writing historical drama—especially at the pace you're aiming for, whether it's completing a screenplay in a weekend or a novel in a week—the secret isn't just talent or passion. It's repetition with refinement. It's doing the work, learning from it, and doing it better next time.

Writing historical drama is one of the most demanding forms of storytelling. You're not just imagining a story—you're recreating a lost world, often under the pressure of accuracy, emotional depth, and narrative complexity. The good news? The more you write, the easier it becomes. Your research muscles get stronger. Your sense of scene, dialogue, and tension gets sharper. And most importantly, your voice becomes unmistakably yours.

So how do you become prolific and keep improving, rather than just churning out forgettable content?

You build a system—and you trust it.

First, set clear writing **cycles**. Start with a one-day draft goal. Then repeat that process weekly or biweekly. Each cycle follows a rhythm: idea generation, outlining, writing, revising, and reflecting. The key isn't how many words you write—it's how often you finish what you start. Completion gives you clarity. It lets you see what worked and what didn't. It builds confidence. Use ChatGPT to accelerate each step: "Give me a historical drama outline in 10 scenes," or "Help me revise this scene to strengthen the emotional arc."

Once a project is complete, take a day to **review and reflect**. What scene flowed best? Which character felt underwritten? Did the setting feel alive? Where did you get stuck? Ask ChatGPT to help analyze: "What's missing in this character's journey?" or "What themes are suggested in this draft that could be developed more next time?" Reflection is how you turn raw output into growth.

Then move right into the next project. Don't wait for the muse to show up. Your momentum is your muse. The more consistently you write, the more ideas will naturally surface. Your mind starts to think in narrative arcs. Your eye notices historical angles everywhere. A newspaper article, a line in a book, or a documentary scene becomes fuel for the next story. Capture those sparks immediately. Keep a running list of historical what-ifs and emotional seeds. Prompt yourself: "What would it feel like to lose your voice during the French Revolution?" or "What story hides behind this 200-year-old photo of a soldier and his dog?"

Improvement also comes from **micro-practice**. In between full drafts, write short scenes or character studies. Use ChatGPT to create mini-prompts: "Write a 200-word monologue from a child hiding in a castle tower during a siege," or "Describe the morning routine of a woman in a leper colony in medieval France." These bite-sized exercises train your speed, your emotional intuition, and your historical accuracy all at once.

Don't get hung up on perfection. That's not the goal. Prolific writers create first, then perfect over time. The more drafts you complete, the more you'll see patterns. You'll start to recognize your weaknesses—maybe you tend to rush endings, over-explain dialogue, or underuse symbolism. Use each new project to focus on one craft element: stronger tension, deeper character arcs, richer world-building. Ask ChatGPT for focused guidance: "How do I build more suspense into this chapter?" or "What sensory details could bring this battlefield scene to life?"

Another key to becoming prolific is building **creative stamina**. Set time blocks. Use writing sprints. Try 25 minutes on, 5 minutes off. If you feel stuck, switch tools. Talk through the scene with ChatGPT. Ask, "What's the emotional center of this moment?" or "What's a better way to express this character's regret without dialogue?" These small conversations keep you engaged and energized.

As you gain speed and insight, build a **portfolio mindset**. You're not just writing a story. You're building a library. Each historical drama you complete becomes part of a growing body of work—each story deepening your voice, widening your range, and sharpening your vision. Some stories will be quiet. Others explosive. Some will stretch over centuries. Others will focus on a single day. And all of them will teach you something new.

Eventually, your process becomes second nature. You'll write faster, but you'll also write deeper. You'll rely less on outside validation and more on internal mastery. You'll know how to start strong, build momentum, and land your story with emotional force—all without second-guessing yourself at every turn.

Use repetition as your teacher. Use reflection as your guide. Use ChatGPT as your creative partner. But above all, use *action* as your rhythm. Finish, learn, write again.

Because the only difference between a writer with one good historical story and a writer with dozens of great ones...is the decision to keep going—again and again—with courage, focus, and just a little fire in your gut.

I hope you found inspiration within these pages. If you liked this book, please leave a review where you bought it. Thank you from the author.

www.ingramcontent.com/pod-product-compliance
Lightning Source LLC
LaVergne TN
LVHW082347200926
848481LV00012B/3489